ABRIDGED PROCEEDINGS

CURE's INTERNATIONAL CONFERENCE

HUMAN RIGHTS AND PRISON REFORM

New York International Hostel
October 6-11, 2001

CONTENTS

A MESSAGE FROM CURE'S EXECUTIVE DIRECTOR:

Dear Friends,

The review of the major human rights documents passed by the United Nations, at the *CURE International Conference on Human Rights and Prison Reform,* produced many suggestions for prison reform. For years, we have been saying that prison abuses violate human rights. Now, we can say what specific article in what specific document is violated. These suggestions for reform should be used in litigation, legislation and education.

The foundation of these documents is the *Universal Declaration of Human Rights* which the UN passed in 1948. This has been called "the bill of rights for the world." In addition, we recommend (1) *A World Made New: Eleanor Roosevelt and the Universal Declaration of Human Rights*, by Mary Ann Glendon (Amazon.com has this book for about $20), and (2) *Human Rights for ALL: A Booklet About Prisoners' Rights,* by C.E. Cypser (to receive a copy send five dollars to National CURE).

This Abridged Proceedings is a classic work and should be used as a textbook in criminal justice courses. We would like to thank the Jane Addams College of Social Work at the University of Illinois in Chicago for their financial assistance in the printing. The College also co-sponsored the Conference.

The CURE international network for prison reform now includes 33 countries. We would like to thank the participants from the twenty-four countries* who attended the Conference, and those from nine other countries who designated delegates and tried but could not obtain a visa or afford to come** (Inputs from some of the latter are nevertheless included in these Proceedings). There must be a next step for this community and the energy generated by the Conference. *We would appreciate your realistic ideas on where we should go from here.*

Sincerely,

Charles Sullivan
Executive Director
National CURE

*Burundi, Brazil, Cameroon, Canada, France, Germany, India, Ireland, Japan, Malawi, Mexico, Mozambique, Paraguay, Peru, Philippines, Portugal, Republique Democratique du Congo, Russia, Switzerland, Trinidad & Tobago, Uganda, United Kingdom, United States, Yugoslavia.

**Argentina, Bangladesh, Benin, Iran, Kenya, Liberia, Nigeria, Pakistan and Zambia.

Chapter I.
Overview

I . 1 RECOVERING LEADERSHIP

Jim Megivern, Prof. Emeritus, UNCW, North Carolina, USA

My hope is to set the tone of advocating strongly, that we urge people to take the international documents much more seriously. Recent American provincialism and separatism have allowed many to forget or simply remain ignorant of the extremely important and influential role this country played at the end of World War II. Many are simply unaware of the sad fact that our country has regressed from the higher ethic we endorsed in 1948 with the *Universal Declaration of Human Rights*. We were in the forefront in advocating the protection of all humanity and the pursuit of worldwide justice. We committed ourselves to working to free the enslaved, to assist the exploited, to care for the wounded, and to protect the persecuted. The Covenants and Protocols are the later nuts-and-bolts arrangements for carrying out these high ideals. But since the 1980s a vindictive, punitive mood has soured our politics and obscured the vision we helped to design which was endorsed by the UN.

It is still my conviction that we can learn from our mistakes and return to the higher path, especially if enough of us insist on getting our elected officials to "do the right thing."

I . 2 HUMAN RIGHTS AND U.S. LAW

Prof. Rick Wilson, Washington College of Law, American Univ., Washington, DC, USA

I want to make four points today:

- Human rights standards have been around for a long time, and courts have made use of them in deciding important cases;
- International human rights law is entering our law slowly, but is doing so each day to a greater and greater extent;
- The government of the US, particularly our State Department, is not friendly to this phenomenon and will resist it at every chance, internationally and domestically;
- Activism from the ground up is the answer. Folks like you must begin to use the language and power of international human rights law and principles to argue for change.

Let me review four cases that I think set out these principles and some others that I will mention in conclusion:

In 1980, in Sterling v. Cupp, 290 Or. 611, 625 P.2d 123, the Oregon Supreme Court reviewed a prison case raising an issue about cross-gender searches of inmates. In reaching their decision, the judges relied not only on state law, but on international principles. The judges did not assert that the international human rights principles were binding, but said that the principles expressed the "worldwide concern" of such bodies as the United Nations. These principles, the judges said, are not "constitutional law," but are important as "contemporary expressions of the same concern with minimizing needlessly harsh, degrading, or dehumanizing treatment of prisoners that is expressed" in the Oregon constitution. (625 P.2d at 131). In a footnote with that statement, the Court refers to a number of international human rights documents and principles, including the *ICCPR, Article 7,* which says that "all persons deprived of their liberty shall be treated with humanity and with respect for the inherent dignity of the human person." So, human rights principles have been around in the courts for more that 20 years, even if they are used infrequently by judges.

Let's jump forward now to 1998, to Nevada, where Michael Domingues faced the death penalty for a crime he committed when he was 16 years old. Michael's lawyers went to court and argued that the *ICCPR, in Article 6(5)*, prohibits the execution of anyone under the age of 18 at the time of their crimes. The lawyers correctly argued that the ICCPR is the law in the United States because treaties have the status of federal law. The prosecutor argued that yes, it was the law, but that the U.S. had taken a "reservation," or exception, to the provision on executing juveniles, and therefore the court did not have to follow the rule. The court divided very closely over the issue, three to two, holding that the exception to the treaty applied, and that Michael's life could not be saved by invoking the treaty. Domingues v. Nevada, 961 P.2d 1279 (Nev. SC 1998). Michael's lawyers appealed to the U.S. Supreme Court, and the court ordered the Solicitor General to file a brief on the issue, so the justices were interested. The brief argued that the Court did not need to take the case because the Nevada court's decision was proper, and the Court denied review. 120 S.Ct. 396 (1999). The court may still have to resolve that issue in some future case. Michael, by the way, is still alive, but his appeals are running out.

Also in 1998, a federal court in New Jersey reviewed a law suit about conditions in a private INS detention facility called Esmore, in Elizabeth, New Jersey. The facility held only immigrants awaiting deportation in the immigration courts. The action was brought under an old law that allows foreigners to sue in the United States for violations of their rights under the "law of nations," which means customary international law. Customary international law is like the common law of the world, and is what governments either actually do or have on their books. The judge found that the private facility provided inadequate and unsanitary conditions, that the food was inadequate, and that the residents were subjected to systematic beatings and sexual abuse. This treatment, the judge concluded, violated a customary international norm prohibiting "cruel, inhuman or degrading treatment," and referred to a number of other decisions from courts in the US finding similar violations. Jama v. Immigration and Naturalization Service, 22 F.Supp..2d 353, 363 (D. N.J. 1998). While the judge held that the US government had immunity, the judge also concluded that the guards and managers of the facility, as well as the INS, might be subject to liability for this wrongful treatment. The case was never appealed.

What's important about that case is that the judge applied a broader standard than our own *Constitution's 8th Amendment*, which requires that the treatment be both "cruel and unusual" for the prisoner to prevail. Note that the international standard says that the treatment can be "cruel, inhuman or degrading," which means that the inmate wins if it's any one of those three – cruel, inhuman OR degrading.

Finally, let's look at a case now pending in the U.S. Supreme Court on the legality of the execution of mentally retarded persons. The case is Atkins v. Virginia, which replaced another case on the docket from last term, McCarver v. North Carolina. The Atkins case is important for many reasons, particularly because it looks likely that the Court may overturn the death penalty for retarded persons. This is because many more states have passed laws abolishing the penalty in those circumstances since the last time the Court heard the issue in 1989. However, what we should watch is what they say about international human rights law.

There were two briefs filed in the case that are important. Both "friend of court" briefs argue how important it is that the Court see this as an international case. The first brief was written on behalf of former ambassadors from the U.S. to other countries, and argues that the death penalty is affecting our foreign relations. I read the position as saying "it's bad for business," which may be more important to the Court than the potential loss of one "criminal's" life. The second brief was written by me and submitted in the name of the fifteen countries of the European Union, all usually strong allies of the U.S. The EU brief argues that only two countries in the world, other than the U.S., now execute the mentally retarded – Japan and Kyrgyzstan. The ambassador of Kyrgyzstan complained later that it abolished the practice in 1999, so we're now the last country in the world, other than Japan, to execute the retarded. Will the Court look to international practice in deciding this case, and not just the number of states in the U.S. that have abolished such executions? We'll have to wait to see. So there are these several ways to argue international law, summarized in the cases I have talked about today:

First, there is the use by the Oregon court of international law as a way to understand U.S. law better. It's not that international law is "binding" on the U.S., but that we gain some benefit by referring to the practice of other countries and international bodies in deciding what we want to do under our own law.

Second, there's the argument in the Nevada case of Michael Domingues that a treaty is the law, and that the law is binding on us here at home. That's a forceful argument, but there are lots of exceptions to the argument that the government can invoke to avoid the application of the treaty, such as the use of the "reservation" or exception that led the court to narrowly uphold Michael's conviction.

Third, there's the customary international law argument made by the federal judge in the New Jersey immigration detention case. By applying the customs of nations, the judge was recognizing that sometimes international law is broader and more protective than our own law. The judge also didn't have to use a formal treaty to reach that conclusion, but only had to recognize that protection from "cruel, inhuman or degrading" treatment or punishment is an international custom that must be upheld in the United States. That's really the same argument that is now being made in the U.S. Supreme Court by the European Union in the death penalty case about executing the mentally retarded – the practice of nations simply no longer permits such executions.

You, as grass roots advocates, can make all the difference in the world by arguing for human rights enforcement in all three of these ways. You can argue it's a better way to understand U.S. law, you can argue it's in a binding treaty creating legal obligations, or you can argue it's a custom and practice of all the countries of the world that the US is bound to follow. This battle will be won from the grassroots up, not from the top down – individual judges and legislators will change their views because of your advocacy, and over time, we all believe, we will measure justice in the United States under international as well as domestic perspectives.

Chapter II. The Death Penalty in the Human Rights Documents

II . 1 THE STEPS FOR ABOLITION

Mehdi Ghasemi, Human Rights Monitor, Tehran, Iran

1. Introduction: New Developments

It is very important for us to hear about new developments regarding the abolition of the death penalty; there is a gradual, and firm movement towards the abolition of the death penalty in the world. Amnesty International, in 2001, listed new countries which abolished the death penalty for all crimes, countries such as; Malta, Ivory Coast, Ukraine, Albania, and Bosnia – Herzegovina. Countries such as South Korea, USA (New Hampshire), India, China and Kyrgyzstan did have moves towards abolition.[1] In May 2001 Amnesty International reported that in 2000 the number of abolitionist countries increased and moratoria on executions were established in the Philippines and in the state of Illinois in the USA. A petition for a worldwide moratorium on executions with over three million signatures collected from 146 countries was presented to Kofi Annan, UN Secretary General. At its meeting in May, the UN Commission on Human Rights again passed a resolution calling on those countries which still maintain the punishment "to establish a moratorium on executions with a view to completely abolishing the death penalty." In August the UN Sub–Commission on the promotion and protection of Human Rights passed a resolution condemning the imposition of the death penalty on those aged under 18 years at the time of the offence, recommending that this be established as contrary to customary international law.[2]

As of March 1998, Amnesty International was able to list a majority of states as being abolitionist in law and practice. While ninety- one states retained the penalty, 104 could be considered as having abolished it. Sixty-three states had abolished it for all crimes and another sixteen for ordinary crimes. In addition, twenty-five states could be considered as abolitionist *de facto*, not having carried out any executions in the previous ten years.[3]

---

[1] "The Death Penalty Worldwide: Development in 2000," (London: Amnesty International, May 2001), (AI INDEX: Act 50/001/2001), pp. 3-5.

[2] *Ibid*, summary.

[3] Nigel S. Rodley, *The Treatment of Prisoners Under International Law*, Second Edition, (Oxford: Clarendon Press, 1999) , p. 204.

2. Human Rights and the Death Penalty

2.1 Universal Declaration of Human Rights (1948)

The *Universal Declaration of Human Rights* is silent on the issue of the death penalty, although it was discussed in the context of the consideration of the right to life. The many proposals that were discussed while the *Declaration* was being drafted ranged from those that would have provided for the abolition of the death penalty, at least in peacetime, to those that would have maintained it without qualification as an explicit exception to the scope of the right to life.[1]

The Assembly, by resolution 2857 (XXVI) of 20 December 1971, affirmed that "in order fully to guarantee the right to life, provided for in *Article 3* of the *Universal Declaration of Human Rights*, the main object to be pursued is that of progressively restricting the number of offences of which capital punishment may be imposed, with view to the desirability of abolishing this punishment in all countries."

2.2 Convention on the Elimination of all Forms of Racial Discrimination, (1965)

The *Convention* defines racial discrimination as any distinction, exclusion, restriction or preference based on race, colour, descent, or national or ethnic origin which has the purpose or effect of nullifying or impairing the recognition, enjoying or exercise, on an equal footing, human rights and fundamental freedoms in the political, economic, social, cultural or any other field of public life. David Cole's research in 1998 showed, a regrettable report about the role of race in sentencing; "from 1979 to 1995, only four white men were executed for killing black victims; defendants who kill white victims are much more likely to receive the death penalty than defendants who kill black victims."

2.3 Covenant on Civil and Political Rights (1966)

One of the first, if implicit, statements on the goal of abolition is to be found in the *International Covenant on Civil and Political Rights*, adopted by the General Assembly of the United Nations in 1966. It came into force on 23 March 1976 and 140 countries are now parties to it. *Article 6* declares in its first paragraph: "Every human being has the right to life. This right shall be protected by law. No one shall be arbitrarily deprived of his life." Another restriction is in paragraph 2, "in countries which have not abolished the death penalty, sentence of death may be imposed only for the most serious crimes in accordance with the law in force at the time of commission of the crime and not contrary to the provisions of the present *Covenant* and to the *Convention on the Prevention and Punishment of the Crime of Genocide*. This penalty can only be carried out pursuant to a final judgment rendered by a competent court." This paragraph limits the nature of the offences for which the death penalty may be imposed.[2] Paragraph 3 of *Article 6* talks about the deprivation of life resulting from the crime of Genocide. Paragraph 4, of *Article 6* of the *Convention* states that "Anyone sentenced to death shall have the right to seek pardon or commutation of the sentence. Amnesty, pardon or commutation of the sentence of death may be granted in all cases. Paragraph 5, of *Article*

---

[1] *Ibid*, also Landerer , "Capital Punishment as a Human Rights Issue Before the UN," 4 *Revue des Droits de L'homme – Human Rights Journal*, (1971), pp. 511,513- 18

[2] Nigel S. Rodley, *Ibid*., p. 207.

6 of the *Convention* requires that "Sentence of death shall not be imposed for crimes committed by the persons below eighteen years of age and shall not be carried out on pregnant women. Violation of the 1966 *Convention* criteria has been one of the main challenges in internationally recognized human rights since 1966, and there are some examples in this respect, such as: the Stanford vs. Kentucky case (1989), where the Supreme Court upheld the death sentences imposed on two murderers, who had committed their crime before reaching their eighteenth birthday.[1]

But above all, the *Convention* does have a inherent desire to abolish the death penalty. In paragraph 6 of *Article 6* "Nothing in this article shall be invoked to delay or to prevent the abolition of capital punishment by any state party to the present *Covenant*."

2.4 Convention Against Torture and Other Cruel, Inhuman or Degrading Treatment or Punishment, (1984)

The *Convention Against Torture and Other Cruel, Inhuman or Degrading Treatment or Punishment* is one of the complicated phenomena in human rights documents. The European Court of Human Rights, in Soering, has confirmed that the circumstances of the imposition and execution of the death penalty may fall foul of the *European Convention on Human Rights Article 3*, prohibition of inhuman or degrading punishment.[2] In the Soering case the European Court of Human Rights concluded that the extradition of the applicant to a jurisdiction in which he would face death row would have violated *Article3*, of the *ECHR*.[3]

The positive influences of *Conventions Against Torture*, should be studied in the context of the increasing number of abolitionists. We can see these developments in Europe: the *European Convention for the Prevention of Torture and Inhumane or Degrading Treatment or Punishment (ECPT)* leans towards the abolition of the death penalty. Except for a small number of Central and Eastern European countries which only recently became members of the Council of Europe, capital punishment has been abolished, *de facto* if not *de jure*.[4] One of the positive actions of the *Convention* is establishing the Committee on Human Rights for victims and communication.

2.5 Convention on the Rights of the Child (1989)

Paragraph (a), of *Article 37* requires that: "States Parties shall ensure that: (a) No child shall be subjected to torture or other cruel, inhumane or degrading treatment or punishment. Neither capital punishment nor imprisonment without possibility of release shall be imposed for offences committed by persons below eighteen years of age." This

---

[1] G. Alan Tarr, *Judicial Process and Judicial Policymaking*, 2nd Edition (Belmont, West/Wadsworth, 1998), p. 251-252. Also: Stanford vs. Kentucky, 492 U.S. 361 (1989).

[2] Nigel S. Rodley, *Ibid*, p.206.

[3] Malcolm D. Evans & Rod Morgan, *Preventing Torture, A Study of the European Convention for the Prevention of Torture and Inhuman or Degrading Treatment or Punishment*, (Oxford: Clarendon Press, 1998), p. 68 (see generally, Soering vs. UK, Judgment, 7 July 1989, Ser. A , No. 161.

[4] *Ibid.*, p. 320, see generally, R. Hood, *The Death Penalty: A World Wide Perspective*, (Oxford: Clarendon Press, 1996)

Convention is one of the most important progresses towards protection of the child, and many countries ratified it.

2.6 Second Optional Protocol to the International Covenant on Civil and Political Rights Aiming to Abolish the Death Penalty (1989)

The General Assembly in 1981 received the results of the Sixth UN Crime Congress debate on the death penalty. The governments of Austria, Costa Rica, Italy, the Federal Republic of Germany, Portugal, and Sweden introduced the text of a draft optional protocol to the *International Covenant on Civil and Political Rights* whereby the parties to such a protocol would commit themselves to abolition. The Commission on Human Rights studied the debates on the different proposals, and held many sessions, mainly in 1982–1984, on the proposal submitted to the Sub-Commission on Prevention of Discrimination and Protection of Minorities. Finally the Assembly adopted the unamended text on 15 December 1989. Paragraph 1, *Article 1* of the *Protocol* requires that: " No one within the jurisdiction of a State Party to the present *Protocol* shall be executed." Paragraph 2, *Article 1* of the Protocol states, "Each state party shall take all necessary measures to abolish the death penalty within its jurisdiction.

3. Summary

The abolition of the death penalty is a goal of international human rights law. In fact, human rights treaties treat the death penalty as an explicit exception to the right of life. To achieve these objectives we have to pass the transitional period. The transitional period should be composed of a dynamic agenda, including limitations such as:

- Progressively restricting the number of offences for which capital punishment may be imposed ,
- Death penalty only imposed for the most serious crimes,
- Must be in accordance with the law in force at the time of the commission of the crime,
- Must not be contrary to the other provisions of the covenant or the Genocide Convention,
- Shall not be imposed for crimes committed by persons below 18 years of age and shall not be carried out on pregnant women,
- Any person sentenced to death shall have the right to seek pardon or commutation of the sentence,
- Limitation on the nature of the offences that may still attract the death penalty.

4. Urgent Actions

Urgent actions against the death penalty include: regional arrangements, prevention of extra-judicial and extra-legal, summary or arbitrary executions, solidarity between INGOs, and reforming the criminal systems.

II . 2 CANADIAN ABOLITION AND EXTRADITION LAW

Rick Prashaw, Communications and Youth Justice Coordinator for The Church Council on Justice and Corrections in Canada.

1. Introduction

I want to draw your attention to a remarkable and very recent Supreme Court of Canada decision involving the matter of extradition and the death penalty, a judgment whose language and research drives Canada more than ever into the abolitionist camp and which highlights the invaluable role of the international abolitionist movement in favourably impacting an individual country's political and legal judgments. And I want to issue as well a warning about the need to work not only against the death penalty we all know and oppose but the living or "slow-motion" death penalty when life literally means life with no hope and no possibility of parole.

2. Canada's Record on the Death Penalty, Including Extraditions

Canada officially abandoned the death penalty for almost all crimes in 1976 and for all crimes, including under military law, in 1998. In fact, a double execution in 1962 had been the last year anyone received the death penalty in Canada. That is all well and good, especially when we witness the "killing fields" on death row in countries like the U.S.

Indeed, in a punitive and retributive climate at home, the current Canadian government has been acting more like a "closet abolitionist" state. Abolitionists in Canada know they fight a rearguard action in this regard, with the return of the death penalty only ever "a vote in Parliament away." However, it is interesting to note that the most recent public opinion polls put support for the death penalty at 53 per cent, its lowest majority ever.

2.1 U.S. vs. Burns

I want to highlight this case because, in the words of one Amnesty International spokesperson, it is "breath-taking" in its scope. The president of the Canadian defence bar called it "a brilliant decision that reaffirms to the world that Canada has certain principles that we consider sacrosanct. We respect the laws of other jurisdictions and we deplore crimes of violence, but there are courageous moral lines in the sand, and the Supreme Court of Canada has drawn one."

The *State of Washington* charged two Canadians, Atuif Rafay, and one of his friends, Glen Sebastian Burns, with aggravated first degree murder in the brutal killing of Rafay's parents and sister in 1994. They were both 19 years of age at the time of the killings. They were arrested in neighboring *British Columbia* in 1995. News reports said that they conspired to kill the three family members in order to collect insurance policies worth about $400,000 Canadian (about $233,000 in U.S. funds). The accused maintain that they are innocent and said that a jail confession was coerced. Under an extradition treaty similar to ones that many countries have with foreign governments, Canada had the right but not the duty to seek assurances that neither Rafay or Burns would be executed if found guilty. The Canadian government chose not to seek such assurances. That decision was appealed all the way to the Supreme Court decision handed down in February. With others, the Church Council on Justice and Corrections roundly criticized the government, stating our extradition policy must affirm rather than undermine our country's official policy against the death penalty. We said: "Neither our sense of morality or justice should stop at the 49th parallel. We believe state-sanctioned executions are wrong in every case, for every one, everywhere. We find it incongruent for a government to say it will not carry out executions in this country but will hand over Canadians to another country who will execute them." Our press release also urged remembering and honouring the victims of these murders in positive ways that do not perpetuate the cycle of violence, as the death penalty does.

In an unanimous [9 - 0] ruling that emphasized the fallibility of the criminal justice system worldwide and the increasing number of wrongful convictions, the country's top court said Canada must seek assurances the death penalty will not be imposed on suspects -- Canadians or any other nationality -- it extradites for trial abroad."

The Supreme Court ruled "*In the absence of exceptional circumstances, assurances in death penalty cases are always constitutionally required.*" The Justices did not define "*exceptional circumstances,*" although they did say that such instances "*would be rare.*" Their decision was based on Section 7 of the *Canadian Charter of Rights and Freedoms,* which deals with "*fundamental justice*". It "*applies because the extradition order would, if implemented, deprive the respondents of their rights of liberty and security of the person since their lives are potentially at risk.*"

The court cited "*...recent and continuing disclosures of wrongful convictions for murder in Canada, the United States and the United Kingdom provide tragic testimony to the fallibility of the legal system.*" They named, as examples, five Canadians wrongfully convicted of murder and released in recent years: Donald Marshall, David Milgaard, Guy Paul Morin, Thomas Sophonow and Gregory Parsons. The court stated that there have been "*factual developments*" since 1991, when it had ruled in favor of the unconditional extraditions of two U.S. fugitives: Charles Ng and Joseph Kindler. These developments included an increased awareness of the frailties of the justice system and more wrongful convictions uncovered. They declared that their ruling applied to citizens of all countries being extradited from Canada; the citizenship of Rafay and Burns was a marginal issue. Their youth was also considered "*of limited weight.*"

The ruling cited the respondents' fundamental message: the death penalty is so horrific, the chances of error are so high, the death row phenomenon is so repugnant, and the impossibility of correction is so draconian that it is simply unacceptable that Canada should participate, however indirectly, in its imposition.

In extraordinary language, the Supreme Court justices found that the death penalty is contrary to the principles of fundamental justice. The unconditional extradition of Mr. Burns and Mr. Rafay to face the death penalty would shock the Canadian conscience. In finding that the death penalty is contrary to the principles of fundamental justice, the Court highlighted that it is final and irreversible and has been described as arbitrary and of doubtful value as a deterrent. "An extradition that violates the principles of fundamental justice will always shock the conscience," the judges concluded.

3. Highlight Court Reasoning and Research

It was as if the Supreme Court was reminding all Canadians, including the government, to be who we say we are. Canada's principled abolition of the death penalty at home, and its spirited advocacy of abolition internationally, confirm Canadian acceptance of abolition as a fundamental principle of our criminal justice system. I do recommend a complete reading of the judgment to get the full breadth of the reasoning and current international research cited in this judgment. The justices did their homework. Http://www.lexum.umontreal.ca/csc-scc/en/pub/2001/vol1html/2001scr1_0283.html.

They cited the many wrongful convictions surfacing in Canada, U.S. and The United Kingdom as tragic testimony to the fallibility of the legal system. "This history weighs powerfully in the balance against extradition without assurances when fugitives are sought to be tried for murder by a retentionist state, however similar in other respects to our own legal system."

3.1. Death Row Phenomenon - The judgment explores this phenomenon related to the lengthy delays brought on by satisfying that the conviction is not wrongful. There are several studies cited on psychological trauma to death row inhabitants. There is reference to a Jamaica decision of 1993, noting the "instinctive revulsion against the prospect of hanging a man after being under the sentence of death for many years." It is an inhuman act to keep a man facing the agony of execution over a long extended period of time. Recent studies in the United States say a state review in death penalty cases averages five years and, in federal cases, the average is 11.2 years. Thirty five per cent of those committed to death row in Florida attempted suicide within a recently studied period.

3.2. European Court of Human Rights, (Soering, 1989). This case points to the irrefutable fact that extradition is a necessary link in the chain of causation that leads, potentially, to the death penalty being administered.

3.3. European Commission on Human Rights, (Altun, Germany, 1983). Often, justice in a foreign country so shocks the conscience that it makes a decision to surrender a fugitive for trial, one that breaches the principles of fundamental justice. "Shocks the conscience" is not to be equated with opinion polls. In the Constitutional Court of South Africa, (S. vs. Makwanyane, 1995), those who are entitled to claim this protection included the social outcasts and marginalized people of our society. It is only if there is willingness to protect the worst and weakest amongst us that all of us can be secure that our own rights will be protected.

3.4. The European Convention on Extradition, signed in 1957, is virtually identical to *Article 6* of the Canada–U.S. treaty, and to *Article 4d* of the *Model Treaty on Extradition* passed by the General Assembly of the UN in Dec.1990, which states that extradition may be refused.

3.5. UN Commission on Human Rights Resolution (1999 and 2000) calls for the abolition of the death penalty and, in terms of extradition, reserves explicitly the right to refuse extradition in the absence of effective assurances from relevant authorities of the requesting State that capital punishment will not be carried out.

4. Lingering Challenges

We all need to do our work in our own countries in terms of abolition and, as we hear of this extraordinary Canadian Supreme Court case, to remember the power in being in solidarity internationally with all who work for abolition of the death penalty. It was the labour, research, studies and judgments made in many countries that the Canadian justices relied on for their unanimous and breath-taking decision in favour of Canada becoming genuinely an abolitionist state.

II . 3 DEATH ROW CONDITIONS IN JAPAN

Maiko Tagusari, Center for Prisoners' Rights, Japan

I'm a member of Center for Prisoners' Rights and Forum 90. CPR and Forum 90 are both Tokyo based civic organizations aiming at the abolition of the death penalty. March 1993, 3 people were executed after 40 months suspension. Since then, the Ministry of Justice has continued executions twice a year.

Since March 1993, the Ministry of Justice has executed 39 death-row inmates, including a 70-year-old man, a person who had serious mental disease, and a man who was 19 years old when he committed the crimes which resulted in capital punishment. In particular, after the Tokyo Subway Gas Attack allegedly committed by the Aum Shinrikyo cult, the current trend to demand harsh punishment for criminals has escalated and more and more people have been sentenced to death. As of today, there are 56 convicted death-row inmates in Japan. This is the highest level in decades.

After the sentences have been confirmed, death-row prisoners are basically prohibited from communication with people outside other than their immediate family and attorneys. The Ministry of Justice says that death-row inmates must accept their coming death calmly and communication with people outside will disturb their minds. Therefore, even family members might be refused if the detention center authorities regard communication with them as inappropriate for the mental stability of the prisoners, as in Ajima's case. Meetings with not only family members but attorneys are monitored and limited to a maximum of 30 minutes. Under such conditions, it's nearly impossible to defend our clients competently. Moreover, in detention centers, death-row prisoners are not allowed to contact other inmates at all. They are completely isolated.

The lack of notification concerning the date and time of the execution is another problem. Death-row prisoners are suddenly notified of their execution only 60 minutes before the execution time. Of course their family or attorneys are never notified before the execution. Now, every morning death-row prisoners in Japan are afraid of being executed. The situations surrounding them are definitely inhumane.

There is no means to contest the legitimacy of the executions prior to its taking place. Seeking retrials is a *de facto* means to escape executions. Criminal Procedure Law says that only the loss of consciousness or pregnancy are suitable grounds for postponing the execution. Even so, until 1999 no one in the course of a retrial procedure had been executed for nearly a half century. Therefore the number of those who file actions for retrial increased and now half of the 56 death-row prisoners are seeking retrial.

However, the Ministry of Justice says that it is possible to execute prisoners who are seeking retrials if they have repeatedly filed similar requests, which have already been rejected. If this procedure were followed consistently, Mr. Sakae Menda, who made requests for retrial 6 times and was finally found not guilty, wouldn't be here with us today.

In 1998, the Japan Federation of Bar Associations issued an official letter to the Prime Minister, demanding suspension of current illegal executions (this means all executions in Japan). They are totally incompatible with ICCPR. But we have not received any response to this letter.

The severe problem we have now is that even legal professionals in Japan don't recognize the cruel, inhuman situations surrounding death-row prisoners. So we need to educate judges and attorneys, so that they can recognize how harsh the conditions in death row are. We do need your cooperation to pressure them and the Japanese government

II . 4 DEATH ROW PRISONERS, THEIR FAMILIES AND FRIENDS

Audry Kaufman, LifeLines Ireland

I chair an organisation called LifeLines Ireland. We are a voluntary, apolitical and non-religious organisation that befriends people on death row in the USA, Caribbean, Zambia and Nigeria through letter writing. Unlike Amnesty International this is on a 1:1 basis.

The death penalty in Ireland was removed from the statute books in 1990 and replaced by a mandatory 40-year sentence for capital murder. On June 7th 2001, the Irish people voted to remove all references to capital punishment from the Constitution.

LifeLines began in the United Kingdom in 1987. Jan Arriens, from Cambridge, was watching a BBC television documentary programme that covered the last days and execution in Mississippi of a young Black man, Edward Earl Johnson. Jan was so moved by the dignity and compassion of the other death row prisoners, who were also in the documentary, that he wrote to the BBC for their names and addresses. As a consequence Jan wrote to all the men and all three responded. In 1991, Paul Cunnigham established LifeLines Ireland. Two years later Paula Hagan developed it as an autonomous group.

Letters are the windows from the free world reaching in to a world of isolation, deprivation and loneliness. A letter in prison means that you do exist, that you are not forgotten and that someone cares enough to spend a little time with you. Letters bring hope; they allow you to feel again, to care about others, above all, to be a person once more and enter into natural dialogue, a dialogue in which you are listened to, one that we in the free world take for granted.

Levels of communication, on both sides, vary from words awkwardly printed and laboured over to the finest flow of prose. Poems, articles, stories, art and craft-work, even books reflect the aspirations and disappointment of those who live on death row. Physical confinement, facing death daily, and the loss of friends cause in-depth self-examination. Pity is the last thing a prisoner desires.

Domingo Cantu had written: "I may be shut away from society but my mind and thoughts still grasp to the free world and to the life I had once in the past. I would like to keep this part of my life alive. So please write." I knew of Domingo as he use to write articles for our newsletter and he also corresponded with a friend of mine. Last year the State of Texas ended his life.

When an escape was foiled in Texas some time back, the prison even took it out on the women. Waking them up every hour during the night to ask them their prison number. At one stage they were made to walk down the corridor in underwear whenever they were taken to the shower. Housed very near to the women on death row were women who had psychiatric problems. On several occasions the latter group of women would be noisy and confused, so to 'quieten' them the guards would 'pepper' spray them. Cathy and Pamela on the row explained how they also suffered side effects, like stinging eyes, from stray spray that came down the corridor.

In Trinidad visits are only 15 minutes even if the visitor has come from outside the country. And so it goes on. Wherever the prison and visitor is - Ireland, the UK, Trinidad or the USA, to name a few - we are always made to feel totally unwanted, and often made to queue for a long time.

A man that I visited has deep scars on both wrists – they had just healed up once again. When he is handcuffed from behind, the manacles cut into the flesh. The elbow joints are stiff from an old wound so he cannot bend them. The scars have accumulated over the years he has been in the system. From time to time he wins, and then the doctor advises that he is to be cuffed in front, maybe because they do not want the wounds to become infected. To date his voice has not been heard, and the daily abuse goes on. He is not even allowed bandages to stop the metal searing into the flesh. When I saw his wrists, I could not believe that anyone could abuse another human so blatantly.

Between the words we hear how the prison system destroys individuals. Violence and power only create an illusion of power and worth; they fail to accomplish anything beneficial. This is why it is important to encourage people, on both sides of the bars, to keep writing because we can never know where and when our words will be heard. If we write enough someone will hear us in the end and, like this conference, we can make a difference.

Freedom Beyond Reach

Freedom can be seen
In a patch of blue sky,
In a fluff of white cloud,
In a tree on the horizon.

Freedom can be heard
In the sigh of the wind,
In the whisper of cooling rain,
In the cry of a soaring hawk.

Freedom can be felt
In the laugh of a cherished visitor,
In the emotion of a loving letter,

In the quiet of a dream-filled night.

And freedom remains beyond
The razor-wire atop fences,
the concrete walls and steel bars,
The outstretched grasp of desperation.

 - Executed in Texas on April 2, 1997 by lethal injection.

Lifelines Ireland: http://homepage.eircom.net/~lifelines/Lifelines.htm

THE FOLLOWING TWO ITEMS ARE TAKEN FROM NOTES OF THE CONFERENCE BY KAY PERRY.

II . 5 ***Anne-Charlotte Dommartin, Ensemble Contre la Peine de Mort, France.***

Serbia and Belarus are the only European countries that still have the death penalty. The Council of Europe will not admit any country that has the death penalty. Japan and the United States currently have observer status with the European Council. That status will be suspended by 2003 if the death penalty is not abolished.

The European Union writes letters to the governor, with copies to the White House and the State Department, every time someone is executed. (Those letters are available at the website: www.eurunion.org.) They also file *amici curiae*. Information on such cases can be sent to the Washington, DC office of the European Union.

Article 20 of the Convention Against Torture has been used successfully against Turkey and Egypt in dealing with torture issues. *Article 21* is not used, because it is perceived to be too much of an attack.

There is a Pakistani Special Rapporteur who has dealt with death penalty issues. She considers only urgent appeals. To date, she has dealt with the issue of minimal standards of protection. If the UN were to receive many complaints, they would likely set up a new mechanism. The Special Rapporteur has considerable freedom to pursue issues of focus.

II . 6 *Nevena Vuckovic-Sahovic, Yugoslav Child Rights Centre, Yugoslavia.*

In Europe, we use International Law extensively. The Federal Republic of Yugoslavia (Serbia and Montenegro) adopted a new penal code which no longer mentions the death penalty, so it is abolished. One country has the death penalty, but it isn't used. They are very concerned about the execution of children and pregnant women. International law forbids that.

The Geneva Convention prohibits the execution of anyone who commits a crime when s/he is less than 18 years old or greater than 70 years old. The African Convention prevents the execution of anyone who commits a crime when less than 18 years old. Asia has no human rights documents.

II . 7 EXCERPTS FROM THE CONFERENCE REPORT CARD

FOR BRAZIL. Brazil has no death penalty, but too many end up dying in prison because of lack of health-care, contagious diseases, or violence. Black, poor, repeat offenders, women, or immigrant offenders do not enjoy the same rights.

FOR USA: There is increasing evidence that a significant number of those on death row were not afforded the protection of a competent court and competent defense. In many jurisdictions, we do not insist that the defense attorney have any experience, competence, or resources needed for capital litigation.

Many states continue to execute those with varying degrees of mental illness, particularly when the accused is suffering from mental retardation or extremely limited mental competence.

Race is an unfair aggravating factor in determining the death sentence. The likelihood of receiving a death sentence is much higher if the defendant is black.[2]

Chapter III. Prison Reform in the Covenant on Civil and Political Rights

§10.3 of the Covenant on Civil and Political Rights states that, "The penitentiary system shall comprise treatment of prisoners the essential aim of which shall be their reformation and social rehabilitation."
§14.1 of the Covenant on Civil and Political Rights states that, "All persons shall be equal before the courts and tribunals. In the determination of any criminal charge against him, everyone shall be entitled to a fair and public hearing by a competent, independent and impartial tribunal established by law."

III . 1 REHABILITATION : ALTERNATIVES & POST RELEASE

Bruno Van der Maat, President,Observatorio de Prisones - Peru

On the one hand prison authorities do seem overprotective of prisoners when they're under their guard: prisoners seem to be a kind of private property of the authorities. They handle prisoners as if they were mere objects, stored in the prison for a while. Everything is decided for them: how to behave, when to get up, when and where to go to sleep, what to eat, what to read, which television programme to watch, with whom to sleep, what illness one can get, to whom one may write, etc. One could argue on the motivation of prison authorities why they do this (some will invoke rehabilitation, others talk about security), but one cannot deny that this is the way they all act. The prisoner is treated like

[2] *United States of America, Rights for All,* Amnesty International, NY, 1998, p.109.

an immature child that cannot and should not decide anything for itself. The authority takes charge of all aspects of the prisoner's life, even the most futile. At least that is the way it goes in Peru. This preoccupation does not mean that everything is decided in the interest of the prisoner. Far from that. I am just describing an overprotective attitude of the authorities, not their capacity to prove in practice what they aim at. Meals are unbalanced and poor, medicine is not available, medical, legal and social care are lacking, security can be bypassed by money, etc. The authority presents itself as a father/mother of the prisoner, but acts as the caricature of a real stepfather/mother.

Once the prisoners are out, the supposedly protective father/mother turns out to be a mere (and bad) stepfather/mother. Even if the prisoner is still under the official control of the authorities, he/she just does not count anymore. Once you are out of prison, you are back in the jungle, where nobody will help you, not even the people who are paid for it. Prisoners get out without a cent (the regimentation that provided the inmate should be saving during his term has just been suspended for seven months for a remake before even coming into force). Many times they don't even have their personal documents. And, worst of all, they have not been prepared to leave. Elbert, an Argentinean lawyer says: preparing a prisoner for free life in a prison is just like trying to teach a person to play football in an elevator. There is no sign of rehabilitation, not even of any preparation for release. Apparently, the overprotective parent is not worried about what will happen to his stepchild once he leaves "home".

In the men's prison where I volunteer, prisoners are released after 7 o'clock in the evening to prevent corrupt lawyers from charging prisoners-to-be-released for their release (by asking them money to "arrange" their release which anyway has already been ordered by the judge, but the prisoner is unknowing of that fact). That means that they leave prison (about 5 miles away from any urban developed center) at night, without a penny and many times even without their personal belongings (which they had to "give away" to their needy and unhappy fellow-inmates). It is difficult to think of a worse way to begin life as a free person.

What we can do is lend a helping hand. First of all we try to (re)establish and maintain the relation between the prisoner and his/her family. We receive letters at our PO Box from people who want to contact the prisoners and vice-versa. This is not always appreciated by the authorities who prefer that the prisoners not have any communication at all, so they do not mix anymore with their "criminal" environment. We also have a radio programme three nights a week, where inmates can send their letters, regards and ask for their favorite song. They can hear this programme in their cells and their family or friends can phone the programme and send their wishes and greetings directly on air. That enables a mother to hear the voice of her child telling her he's ok at school, for example. Or an inmate may listen to his girlfriend telling him she'll wait for him. etc. This kind of programme maintains relations, especially when distances are large and there's no money to travel.

In association with the local Prison Fellowship (PF) Association, inmates can ask to go to a transit house, operated by PF in our city. They're provided with lodging for a limited time, but not with food. They have to leave everyday to find work and earn their meal. The home also tries to accompany them by having volunteers to speak to. What is strange is that many times the prison authorities have not accepted the address of this transit house as a guarantee to let prisoners out.

We have a plan to prepare inmates for their release by organizing some group-meetings with them in prison in order to inform them of the post-release situation: the necessity of saving before leaving, contacts, how to prevent having problems etc.

III . 2 HUMAN RIGHTS AND PRISON REFORM IN D.R .CONGO

Ghighi Poshi Frangoie, R.D. du Congo

The JURIS Center, an NGO composed of religious professionals of different faiths as well as experienced laity, has been working for two years on a project concerning rights of defense and the prisoner.

1. Statement of Principles

The prisoner does not lose all his rights as a human person, except those that are stated expressly in the conviction. In accordance with the minimal regulations for the treatment of convicts in the Economic and Social Council of the UN, the convicted has the right to be rehabilitated, reclassified, and prepared to return to free society.

1.1 Preview of the Congolese Penitentiary System

The present Congolese penitentiary system is characterized by a lack of qualified personnel, an insufficiency of infra-structures, and obsolescence of related laws. Consequently, the jail is a place of massive violations of human rights. Some of these are:

- an irregular and insufficient feeding;
- an intolerable promiscuity encouraging some various sexual violations;
- delays of preventive detention in margin of the law;
- precarious hygienic and sanitary conditions;
- the absence of a program of "resocialisation", so that most of the delinquents leave jails with a more criminal predisposition.

2. Program of the JURIS Center

The plan of action of the JURIS Center includes various directions, notably of sensitizing the general public, efficient help to prisoners, and the development and adoption of a code of law to reform the Congolese penitentiary system.

2.1 Informing the Public

We realize that informing the general public and the authorities on prison realities as well as on the necessity of reforms, are indispensable to getting a better protection of human rights and society. Information is by conference proceedings and posters. We foresee the publication of booklets and more regular visits in jails in the company of decision-makers and legislators. An important asset is the collaboration of the archdiocese of Kinshasa of which many religious and laity are members of our organization and have already worked with us. Certain Protestant churches are also interested in the abolition of the death penalty. The collaboration of local jail chaplains is also assured. We maintain good relations with the press and numerous local NGOs.

2.2 Help to Prisoners

Help to prisoners is modest, and our wish is that it will become more consistent and more useful, not only to prisoners, but also to the state. At present we supply free judicial aid to those prisoners deprived of all defense, through magistrates and lawyers who are members of our organization. Those of our members in the legal profession endeavor whenever possible to deliver information to those who need it. We also supply material aid, food, clothing, and quality medical care. Those who are distant from their families have a right to hear from them, notably by phone and letters, and the bill is paid by voluntary organizations. There is also a new program for schooling and job training, by specialists in the field.

2.3 Legal Projects to Reform the Penitentiary System

Our specialists have been working on the development of a legal project which aims at the reform of the Congolese penitentiary system, striving to modernize it. The existing texts date for the most part, back to colonial times and are not adaptable to the present level of penitentiary science, nor to the evolution of the prison population, nor to the money available to the jail system. The project will be sustained by lobbying in conjunction with other NGOs.

III . 3 EDUCATION IN THE PHILIPPINES AND THE UNITED NATIONS DOCUMENTS ON HUMAN RIGHTS ON EDUCATION.

Fr. Anthony J. Ranada, S.V.D. Jail Chaplain, Philippines

The Philippines (population75million) has free elementary and secondary schooling for its youth. However, only 45 out of 100 Grade 1 entrants finish high school and 65 finish elementary. Problem: more students (55%) drop out than graduate from high school.

Thus, the Bureau of Non-Formal (Alternative) Education was set up to complete the basic education of youth/adults that dropped out of the formal school system. It's the poor (Philippine poverty line is 40%) who go to free public schools for their basic education the quality of which suffers in comparison with private schools who cater to the middle class and the elite classes having high tuition fees with quality education.

1. Alternative Learning System. Non-Formal Education Accreditation & Equivalency System (NFE-A&E). is a non-formal education program which provides an alternative means of learning and certification for out-of-school youth and adults 15 years old and above, who are unable to avail of the educational opportunities of the formal school system, or who have dropped out of formal elementary and secondary education. The focus is on functional, not academic learning as in the formal system.

Education is leading a person from the known to the unknown, to start where he is and chart the course for greater knowledge and maturity. Thus it aims to provide a system of levels of literacy and non-formal learning achievement, offers an alternative pathway of learning, and enables the target learners to gain reading, writing and numerical skills.

The curriculum framework has five learning strands: 1) Communication Skills, 2) Problem Solving and Critical Thinking, 3) Sustainable Use of Resources, 4) Development of Self & Sense of Community, and 5) Expanding One's World Vision (peace & non-violent resolution of conflicts).

2. Correctional Education in Jails

Non-Formal & Alternative Education is the Direction for Correctional Education in the Philippines. Prison and prisoners being what people judge them to be, we really have to change the retributive approach to a Restorative Justice Philosophy, so people in government and in the private sector may be more willing to allocate resources to correctional or re-integrative education.

Since people in jail may truly have committed crime or were falsely accused but are thought to have committed crime, this level of consciousness must be addressed to formulate a non-formal educational strategy specific to prisoners as opposed to out-of-school youth and adults living outside prison walls and relatively free to move around.

The advantage in non-formal education is its lack of coercion compared with the formal. There is a built-in compulsion in formal basic education as well as in the pursuit of higher education. There may be the deep desire to learn in students doing non-formal education, which is lacking in outside students who have many other competing interests that make them skip school.

Robert K. Greenleaf in Servant Leadership has this to say about prisons: "We now realize that penal institutions, other than focusing on the retributive vengeance of society and restraining anti-social actions for a period, do very little to rehabilitate. In fact, they dehabilitate and return more difficult offenders to society." Will not a sense of involvement in community (not in divisive and deadly gangs) enhance the learning motivation and skills of the inmate apart from many other benefits? The Instructional Manager must make sure this sense of community is instilled in the inmate-learners. A heart at peace and on fire leads to a mind eager to learn.

The balance between the facilitating role of the instructional manager and the self-learning of the learner may follow the words of St. John the Baptist: "I (Instructional Manager) *must decrease* and he (Learner) *must increase.*" The learner progresses from 1st Level (Basic Literacy-Illiterate) through the 2nd Level of Semi-Literate at Elementary Stage to the 3rd Self-Learning Level at the Secondary Stage, when learning and education become *self-propelling.*

III . 4 COGNITIVE BEHAVIORAL EDUCATIONAL PROGRAMS.

Janine Edmonds, CURE-ENOUGH, Michigan, USA

In the USA, we now find about 20 different types of cognitive-behavioral educational programs. Each attempts to change behavior by changing dysfunctional ways an individual thinks. They aim to bring automatic thinking habits under the individual's control, in the belief that criminal acts are committed by "thinking without really thinking." These programs teach *how* to think, not *what* to think.

The basic steps of the cognitive-behavioral programs vary from program to program. Three key steps for participants are:

Step One: Learn to objectively observe their internal thoughts and feelings, attitudes, and beliefs.

Step Two: Learn to recognize particular thinking that has led them to criminal acts. They recognize their behavior is not due to external circumstances, but their own thinking. They realize that they can control their thinking.

Step Three: Practice new thinking. They are challenged to find their own new ways of thinking in real life situations. Typically they also will alter some of their basic beliefs and attitudes toward life.

Seven basic ground-rules for implementation of these programs are:

Time	Programs may vary in length from weeks to years, often 2-3 times each week with homework in between sessions. There are different levels of readiness. After-care and follow-up are needed. It's a slow process.
Motivation/ Buy-in	At higher security facilities, inmates must take such classes in order to move to a lower security-level facility. In some facilities, lump sum payments are given. In some facilities, the classes are conditions for eligibility for job programs.
Instructors	Requires group leadership skills and enthusiasm. Instructors need to "know themselves and use the thinking skills automatically themselves." They need to be objective, non-judgmental, and versed in multi-cultural diversity. They must have the skill to challenge participants which creates discomfort, anxiety, and sometimes anger, which may be required for change.
The group	The size of the group is between 8 and 15. It needs to be cohesive, interactive, participatory and cooperative. The program may exist on video.
Thinking & Behavior	Patterns of thinking must be identified individually, and a plan for change must be developed for each individual.
Transferable	There is a need to apply all this to real life situations, for repeated practice, and for support from family, fellow inmates, and staff.
Cognitive Interventions	Interventions should be systematic with demands for new self-awareness.

There are great and fundamental differences in the relationships among inmates, staff and officers, in cognitive-behavioral programs and business as usual programs. Some of these differences are:

COGNITIVE-BEHAVIORAL PROGRAMS	**'BUSINESS AS USUAL' PROGRAMS**
Teachers, staff as facilitators; an *educational* program with teaching and learning.	Therapy programs using psychology staff; a *therapy* program.
Trained Correctional Officers are part of the process as a defining characteristic of the program. A joining of programs, rehabilitation, and security. Officers become the most effective advocates.	Security vs. Programming: Security always wins.
Inmates develop self-determination and are in conscious control of their own lives. Raising consciousness of responsibility.	Deleterious effects of the harsh prison environment on inmates.
Program is confrontational and sets high standards of performance, but does not attempt to coerce compliant behavior.	Authorities coerce compliant behavior with threat of lost privileges and punishment.
Focus on offender restoration. Officers become agents of change.	Officers are keepers of order. Focus on authority and coerce compliant behavior. Control.
Training officers to "personalize cooperation by showing a willingness to enter into cooperative relationships with inmates."	Officers are reprimanded if they show a cooperative relationship with inmates.
Focus on cooperative relationships and behaviors. Authority is non-antagonistic.	Us vs. Them. Authority as the enemy. Officers are antagonistic authority.
Staff & officers are trained to understand that communication & related human connections are complex and multi-faceted. The importance of human connections. Omits Us vs. Them.	Officers & staff are the control and focus only on non-compliant behavior. Thus offenders remain defensive and see authority as the enemy.
Expands the role of officers and provides career opportunities and increased job satisfaction.	Negative focus and job dis-satisfaction.

Here are some examples of current cognitive-behavioral programs:

Name	*Research Results*	*Purpose*	*Correctional District*
Cognitive Behavioral Treatment	5 year study: Recidivism 37% for CBT participants vs. 55% non-CBT participants	Systematic, step-by-step process of raising the moral reasoning	Shelby County Correction Center in Memphis, TN
Cognitive Self-Change Training (CSC)	Recidivism reduced 20% more for CSC participants vs. Non.	Process for achieving self-determination and conscious control of their own thinking and choices.	Vermont Correctional System
Reasoning & Rehabilitation (R&R)	R&R reduces recidivism, but level of group is inconsistent.	Changing underlying thoughts and attitudes that lead to criminal behavior	Canada Correctional System, Britain, Colorado

III . 5 TREATMENT OF SEX ABUSERS IN PRISON

Wayne Bowers, Chair, CURE SORT, Michigan, USA

Gerald Blanchard, a therapist of persons who have sexually abused, makes it clear in his book, *The Difficult Connection,* that a vital need in working with a client is to allow that person to sense an atmosphere of reason, a place where he/she may openly discuss some of the most intimate moments in their life. We may not understand or agree with what this person has done, but yet, to help him/her gain a reasoning of a need to curtail certain behavior or change, the person must sense a comfort zone to speak about it. We cannot expect that person to feel comfortable in a confrontive environment, for then the defensiveness and denial that has kept the person in a secret web of silence full of shame will continue.

A therapy session needs to be an open arena to work on issues that need correcting and to change some cognitive concepts that have taken many years to develop.

With this in mind, it is becoming more and more alarming that many prisons require a provision in regards to information stated in a sex abuser counseling session. Statements are made to the prisoners that any information they share could be held against them. It could mean further charges, a pass on a parole hearing, possible reasons to prevent certain improvements in their status in the prison, and most recently, the potential of being held beyond their sentence on the basis they may re-offend.

Reports constantly surface that prisoners are either refusing therapy sessions or refusing to state openly about their case in sessions, with the threat of further penalty being held over them.

There is a need to look at sexual offenses as a public health issue. Those who have a distorted cognitive thinking and relate inappropriately and harmfully in a sexual fashion have serious emotional defects and disorders that need to be addressed in a scientific manner.

III . 6 HUMAN RIGHTS AND PRIVATE PRISONS

Eugene Keyser, CO-CURE, Colorado, USA

The use of private, for-profit, prisons is an example of our government abdicating its responsibility to the general public in order to pander a special-interest group. We ordinarily trust our government to protect and secure the poor, the weak and the powerless in our society, rather than to foster their exploitation and abuse by predator corporations.

Our state government officials unashamedly use these prison corporations as economic development for rural and depressed areas, and the prison corporations often do not provide needed professional treatment, education or medical services to their inmate citizens.

III . 7 EXCERPTS FROM THE CONFERENCE REPORT CARDS

FOR PERU: Only security is aimed at; there are no resources for treatment. For juveniles, there are no resources nor personnel for treatment outside of prison; therefore most juvenile offenders are locked up. Quality legal assistance, for people depending on *pro-deo* defenders is not guaranteed.

FOR YUGOSLAVIA: Laws need to be changed, particularly provisions of the Serbian Constitution. Until October 2000, there were mass illegal arrests of members of opposition parties and others critical of authorities. Since then, only a few have been reported.

FOR BRAZIL: Non judicial but governmental, community-based organs, called "Tutelar Counsels," handle minor and first offense cases. They help with re-socialization and job preparation. Though under-funded, they serve well. In the judicial system, alternatives to incarceration are by law to be primary means; however, in practice incarceration is the primary means.

Many charges are false or exaggerated, especially when there is a prior record.

FOR USA: The judicial system strongly favors those with financial means. The poor, the mentally ill and the mentally retarded are often not provided with competent representation. Racial bias in the selection of criminal charges by police and prosecutors, and in jury selection are all too common.

The correctional system has not made a priority of rehabilitation which would provide the incarcerated with the addiction treatment, psychological counseling, education, life skills, and job training which they need to become productive members of society. Most systems in this country have reduced or given up on rehabilitation.

Despite the evidence that education can reduce recidivism rates, educational programs have been cut and post secondary levels of education have been virtually eliminated by the complete curtailment of Pell grants.[1]

Chapter IV. Universal Suffrage in the Covenant on Civil and Political Rights

§25 of the Covenant on Civil and Political Rights states that, "Every citizen shall have the right and the opportunity:

a. To take part in the conduct of public affairs, directly or though freely chosen representatives;
b. To vote, and to be elected at genuine periodic elections which shall be universal and equal suffrage..."

IV . 1 THE RESULTS OF DISENFRANCHISEMENT

Kenny Linn, J.D., M.L., CURE-Federal, Florida, USA

1. Theory of Re-Enfranchisement

1.1 Reformation of the convicted felon after he has paid his dues: If he has served his time he should have the same opportunities as everyone else to be part of the community, be a taxpayer, be part of the system. Those who have done their time should be fully reinstated, so as to become productive members of their community.

1.2 Christian principles of forgiveness and redemption.

1.3 If we're truly going to pay more than lip service to the idea of rehabilitation of ex-felons, they should get the vote.

2. Statistics on Felon Disenfranchisement

2.1. The Sentencing Project estimates there are 4.2 million people in the USA who are barred from voting because of convictions. This figure includes prisoners, ex-prisoners, probationers, and parolees.

2.2. Only two states presently allow prisoners to vote, Maine & Vermont.

2.3 38 states allow ex-felons to vote.

2.4. But, Florida and 11 other states bar felons from voting for the rest of their lives.
  a. Those other states are MS, AL, VA, KY, IA, NV, WY TN, WA, AZ, & MD.
  b. TN & WA only ban those convicted prior to the 1980s.

---

[1] *Education as Crime Prevention - Providing Education to Prisoners*, The Center on Crime, Communities and Culture, NY, Sept. 1997; At least 25 states have reportedly reduced vocational and technical training for prisoners, and higher education has been largely eliminated

c. Arizona and Maryland only ban two-time felons.

i. There are 217,000 disenfranchised ex-felons in Virginia.

ii. There are 60,000 disenfranchised in Maryland.

iii. Florida disenfranchises at least 647,000 people.

3. Statistics on Minority Disenfranchisement

3.1. 1/3 of all those disenfranchised are blacks although they make up only 14% of the USA population.

3.2. More than ½ of those who can't vote are either Black or Latino.

3.3. 31% of all Florida and Alabama Black men are disenfranchised.

3.4. 26% of all Black men in MS, NM, VA, and WY are disenfranchised.

3.5. 17% of all Black men in MN, NJ, RI, & WI are disenfranchised.

4. Disenfranchisement in Florida

4.1 A felon is banned from voting for life in Florida unless he is granted executive clemency.

4.2 Restoration of civil rights in Florida is a joke. Here is what is involved:

a. The detail of paperwork required by the clemency board would fill two file cabinets with 50 sources, spanning 20 years of a person's life.

b. An applicant must provide copies of a birth certificate, a Social Security Card, any educational certificates, a complete and detailed 20 year residential & employment history, including names of all supervisors, all bank, mortgage and credit details, the previous 3 years of income tax returns, all court documents, all traffic tickets ever received along with proof of payment, and character reference letters.

c. Applicants must have a 10-minute hearing in Tallahassee in front of the Governor & three cabinet members and the decision is left entirely to their discretion.

d. The process takes 2 years, takes vast amount of time and costs thousands of dollars in travel expenses and lost wages.

e. The system is daunting for the illiterate and the poorly educated to have a clemency petition granted.

f. One cannot even begin to apply for re-enfranchisement in FL until ten years after one is off parole.

4.3 Although 647,000 is the 1998 figure for disenfranchised felons in FL, the number now could be as high as ¾ of a million.

5. Disenfranchisement and the Last Election

5.1. The 2000 presidential election was decided by 537 votes in Florida.

5.2. Of the 647,000 disenfranchised in Florida, 400,000 of whom are black, how many would have voted for George Bush?

5.3. Results show that two Congressional seats in Florida, one in Long Beach, CA, two in PA and one in GA were all won by Republicans by a couple of hundred to a couple of thousand votes.

5.4. It is obvious that the overwhelming majority of disenfranchised would have voted Democrat.

5.5. Two seats on the Alabama Supreme Court would have gone Democratic as well if ex-felons had been re-enfranchised there.

5.6. The impact of losing 2-3% of the electorate was devastating to the Democratic Party in the last election and Democrats should sit up and take notice.

6. Some Re-Enfranchisement Changes Since the Last Election

6.1. Last year, Delaware changed from life to a 5-year post-prison waiting period.

6.2. This year, the New Mexico legislature has passed a bill returning the vote after prison release.

6.3. Connecticut has given the vote to those on probation.

6.4. In April, Maryland passed re-enfranchisement in the House & the Senate appointed a task force to study the issue in June.

6.5. Virginia's State Crime Commission established a task force to study the present case-by-case review of each ex-felon by the Governor of the more than 5% of the voting age population now disenfranchised.

   1. VA has more Blacks banned from voting than they have registered to vote.

6.6. Kentucky has passed a new bill that requires the Department of Corrections to help inmates fill out voter paperwork.

6.7. On the federal level, Senator Conyers (MI) and Reid (NV) have authored a bill to allow ex-felons to vote in federal elections.

   1. It failed to pass last Spring, but it will be reintroduced this term.

7. What Needs to be Done

7.1. All lawsuits should argue that it is an 8th Amendment violation and is cruel and unusual punishment to permanently deprive a citizen of the fundamental right to vote after he has completed a sentence that has specific punishment for the crime.

7.2. All lawsuits should argue that it is a violation of *Article 21* of the *Universal Declaration of Human Rights* that states everyone has a right to take part in the government of his country. USA has signed this document.

7.3. All lawsuits should argue it is a violation of the *International Covenant on Civil & Political Rights* that says prisoners should be able to vote.

7.4. All lawsuits should argue that it is a violation of the 14th &15th Amendments to deny ex-felons the vote and the Federal Voting Rights Act of 1965, which disallowed the dilution of minority votes.

7.5. There should be state wide referendums in all states of all voters and potential voters on the issue of re-enfranchisement of prisoners and ex-felons.

IV . 2 FELONY DISENFRANCHISEMENT LAWS IN THE USA

Marc Mauer, The Sentencing Project, Washington, DC, USA

The scale of felony voting disenfranchisement in the USA is far greater than in any other nation and has serious implications for democratic processes and racial inclusion. The impact of these laws has been exacerbated by a quarter century of "tough on crime" criminal justice policies that have led to more people going to prison for longer periods of time. Policy makers at the state and federal level are beginning to reconsider these policies in light of legitimate correctional objectives and the democratic interests served by recognizing the right to vote of all sectors of the population.

- **Connecticut:** In May 2001, the Governor signed into law a bill that extends voting rights to felons on probation. The law is expected to make 36,000 persons eligible to vote.
- **Delaware:** Until recently, Delaware imposed a lifetime voting ban on felons. In June 2000, the General Assembly passed a constitutional amendment restoring voting rights to some ex-felons five years after the completion of their sentence.
- **New Mexico:** In March 2001, the Legislature adopted a bill repealing the state's lifetime ban on ex-felon voting.
- **Pennsylvania:** A Commonwealth Court restored the right to vote to thousands of ex-felons who, as a result, were entitled to vote in the 2000 presidential election.
- **Virginia:** The Virginia legislature passed a law in 2000 enabling certain ex-felons to apply to the circuit curt for the restoration of their voting rights five years after the completion of their sentence; those convicted of felony drug offenses must wait seven years after completion. The circuit court's decisions are subject to the governor's approval.

IV . 3 VOTING BY PRISONERS ?

Betty Cypser, Co-Chair, CURE-New York, USA

First I will state two seemingly accepted ethical propositions:

1. In the holy and just community, human rights should be respected.
2. If a human being is impacted by a law, he should have a part in the formulation of that law.

Most of you will agree to these two propositions. However, I will give two counter objections by those who oppose voting by prisoners. If we leave out the obvious arguments concerning racial disparities, imprisonment and mistreatment of the innocent, invalid imprisonment of the mentally ill and the addicted, etc., and give the further questionable consideration that all prisoners are persons to be punished, how should the holy and just community treat criminals? I believe that justice should be restorative, but many people feel that justice requires punishment. Opponents to my viewpoint propose the two following objections:

1. The criminal has not respected other people's rights, so he should be punished by having his rights taken away.
2. The criminal has broken the law, so obviously does not have the ability to participate in the making of laws.

Let's think about early suffrage in this country. I will give two examples of voting rights in the history of our country.

1. How did we form holy community with the indigenous people of North America in 1620? We roared into their territory, and did not let them vote or allow them to participate in the making of laws.
2. Culturally, women were considered property and so could not (or were believed to be not intelligent enough to) vote or have a part in the formulation of law in this country. This is also still the case in many religious groups, such as the Roman Catholic, where regulations are made by men. This system keeps power in the hands

of a few (who are men). Our Congress is predominantly male, even though there are more women than men in our country.

Next, I am giving two facts:
1. Prisoners are counted in the census, where they are imprisoned.
2. College students can be counted in their home towns or at their college, and can vote by absentee ballot.

Why can't prisoners have a similar choice?

Finally, I have two questions:
1. How can we make voting by inmates palatable to small towns in New York State, who feel that if prisoners voted in local elections, they would take over and run the town?
2. If prisoners were allowed to vote by absentee ballot in their home communities, would it improve the infrastructures and community values in those communities?

Considering these questions, these above facts, objections, and propositions, lets propose a possible vision for the future. CURE has two main objectives:
1. We put in prison only those who need to be there.
2. For those who don't need prison, we attempt rehabilitation in their home community.

In Switzerland they don't have prisons; they just have jails. This situation keeps prisoners in their home communities closer to their families and their children. Both those in-jail and those undergoing alternative sentencing could be doing meaningful work at a just wage. Local churches would be better able to serve the needs of those who ran afoul of the law. They could even supply citizen volunteers to assist parole and probation supervisors. Restorative justice could be applied, rather than retributive justice.

IV . 4 RESOLUTION PROPOSED BY THE CONFERENCE FOR ADOPTION BY THE GENERAL ASSEMBLY OF THE UNITED NATIONS:

"The General Assembly urges all States to commit by this resolution to take all measures necessary to implement universal and equal suffrage in their respective countries, including prompt adoption of such domestic legislation as may be necessary to effectively ensure this fundamental human right for all disenfranchised persons of every status in life, including prisoners and ex-prisoners, in accordance with international human rights obligations and the general welfare of all peoples."

This resolution has been submitted to the various Country Permanent Representatives to the United Nations and to appropriate departments in participating countries.

Chapter V.
Holding Prisons Accountable in the Covenant on Economic, Social and Cultural Rights

V . 1 PRISONERS AND THEIR FAMILIES AND FRIENDS

Dr. Creasie Finney Hairston, Dean, Jane Addams College of Social Work, U. of Illinois, Chicago, USA

United States public policies, not unlike international human rights documents, speak to the importance of the family as a social institution and to the protection of children and their relationships with their parents. Historically, Federal and state correctional communications policies have identified the maintenance of family relationships during imprisonment as a valued social goal. In line with that purpose families and friends are able to visit prisoners in prison, communicate with them via telephone or letters, and sometimes send packages, gifts or money. A few states allow family members to have private, overnight family visits; at least two states permit female prisoners who give birth while incarcerated to keep their infant children with them; and a few states provide alternative, community based settings wherein some women prisoners convicted of nonviolent crimes may serve their time while keeping their young children with them. Family connections and community ties are also recognized as important in policies and practices governing release from prison.

During the past year diverse constituencies, including the President of the United States, politicians, government bureaucrats, and research think tanks have elevated the families and children of prisoners to a new level of public visibility and discourse. Family issues have emerged as priority areas in government sponsored faith based initiatives and prisoner community reentry and reintegration programs. Of particular note is the allocation of Federal monies in September 2001 to community groups to plan, implement, and evaluate programs and services for children of prisoners, and to the Child Welfare League of America to establish a national resource center on the children of incarcerated parents.

There are, at the same time, widespread violations of human rights with regard to prisoners and their families and children. Exploitation of families, degrading and dehumanizing treatment of family members, disregard for family bonds and punishment of children because of the criminal status of their parents are all rather commonplace. Some practices are defended under the banner or guise of institutional security or community safety. Others are simply described as reflecting the public will or as necessary strategies for ridding the community of drugs. Some are subtle and go unnoticed except by those families who endure their impact. Others are more direct and even blatant. Many are sanctioned by the highest levels of government as official policy while others are the result of benign elect.

Ironically, some of the more noticeable examples of human rights abuses have resulted from technological advances that one might expect to support, rather than thwart, family relationships. Telephone use is a prime example. While telephone rates have decreased considerably for the general U.S. population, they have increased at exorbitant levels for families who communicate by phone with incarcerated relatives. These rates are a result of contracts between correctional agencies and telephone companies that guarantee lucrative profits to phone companies and governmental agencies at the expense of families and friends who pay for the collect phone calls from prisoners. As an example, a 30 minute phone call that would cost the general public $1.50 if placed from a residential phone costs the prisoner's family over $30. One prison official advised me that he needed the millions of dollars profit his phone system generated annually to provide mental health services; another told a commission convened to study the situation that the public wanted prisoners' families to pay more for the calls. A third defended his practices to me by reasoning that prisoners' families were dysfunctional.

Technology has also made it relatively easy for corrections officials to disseminate lots of information to the general public. Many departments of corrections display detailed information (pictures, criminal history, current location, etc.) about individual prisoners and former prisoners on their websites. It is not immediately obvious how this type of information display protects the public. It is apparent, however, that these sites serve as a shaming device, subjecting prisoners' children and families to public humiliation.

Many correctional policies and practices devalue parent-child relationships and the cultural traditions and extended family networks of African American families. Some states permit children to visit their incarcerated parents only if the parents are the children's biological parents, or only if a child's custodial parent accompanies him/her on the visit. (In contrast, many African American families rely on different family members to carry out traditional roles of biological parents. A young aunt, rather than the child's parent, may be in the best position to make a long prison visit. Step families, i.e. brothers and sisters residing in the same household with different mothers or fathers, are rather common.) Other states restrict parent-child communication by placing prisoners in prisons that are at great distances from their communities. Visiting is made even more difficult by subjecting visitors to humiliating and demeaning practices. These include visiting waiting areas that provide no access to rest rooms or water, strip searches of visitors without justifiable cause and no recourse for visitors, shackling prisoners though they are separated from visitors by physical barriers, and non-contact visits between parents and their young children.

Post prison policies designed to punish criminals, in particular those with drug offenses, serve the larger purpose of punishing prisoners' parents and children merely because of their association with each other and their desire to maintain a family unit. Among these policies are those that exclude drug offenders from living in public or Federally subsidized housing, from receiving cash assistance, food stamps, and medical care from the government, and from receiving Federal student loans. Since most prisoners are poor, their access to these type resources, often make the difference in terms of whether they are able to provide basic resources for their children and reestablish their households upon release. Since the majority of individuals incarcerated on drug charges are African American, though they are not the majority of drug users, there is a concern regarding racial inequities here as well.

Even a cursory examination of policies and practices governing Federal and state prisoners provides glaring examples of government sanctioned efforts that exploit prisoners' families and negatively impact family maintenance and the well being of children and other family members during and after imprisonment. If the stated purposes of family strengthening and family maintenance, prevention of recidivism, and enhancement of the quality of life for all our children are to be attained, the inconsistencies between the purposes of different pronouncements and the actual policies that are implemented must be addressed. This attention must occur at the highest levels of government and must acknowledge the fundamental human rights of all individuals, the least of these which might very well be prisoners and their children and families.

V . 2 PRISON LABOR

Thomas W. Petersik, Ph.D., Washington, DC, USA

Does the United States, which signed but did not ratify the *International Covenant on Economic, Social and Cultural Rights* (January 3, 1976), meet the requirements of the Covenant?

By denying almost all of the 2 million adults incarcerated in its Federal, state, and local jails and prisons any right to support themselves or their families, the United States may be in significant violation of the *International Covenant on Economic, Social and Cultural Rights.* Moreover, because of its consequences for children, families, and incarcerated individuals, the United States may also be in violation of the United Nations *Universal Declaration of Human Rights.* **This denial has the effect of extending the violation beyond incarcerants to the harm of children, women, and families.**

Essence of the United States Violation with respect to incarcerated persons: Part I, *Article 2* of the *Covenant on Economic, Social, and Cultural Rights* declares, "In no case may a people be deprived of its own means of subsistence." Here are other major parts of the *Covenant* for which the United States may be in violation:

Article 6: "The States Parties to the present *Covenant* recognize...the right of everyone to the opportunity to gain his living by work which he freely chooses or accepts, and will take appropriate steps to safeguard this right, [including]... technical and vocational guidance and training...policies...to achieve steady economic...development and full and productive employment under conditions safeguarding fundamental ...economic freedoms to the individual."

Article 7: "The States Parties to the present *Covenant* recognize the right of everyone to the enjoyment of just and favorable conditions of work which ensure, in particular:

(a) Remuneration which provides all workers, as a minimum, with (i) Fair wages and equal remuneration for work of equal value without distinction of any kind...(ii) A decent living for themselves and their families...
(b) Safe and healthy working conditions;

(c) Equal opportunity for everyone to be promoted in his employment...subject to no considerations other than those of seniority and competence..."

Article 8: "The States Parties to the present Covenant undertake to ensure:

(a) The right of everyone to form trade unions and join the trade union of his choice...for the promotion and protection of his economic...interests. No restrictions may be placed on the exercise of this right other than those prescribed by law and which are necessary in a democratic society in interests of national security or public order or for the protection of the rights and freedoms of others;

(d) The right to strike, provided that it is exercised in conformity with the laws of the particular country.

Article 13: "The States parties to the present *Covenant* recognize the right of everyone to education...to the full development of the human personality and the sense of its dignity [to]...enable all persons to participate effectively in a free society..."

Critical components of the *Universal Declaration of Human Rights* also identify U.S. areas of violation:

Article 23: (1) Everyone has the right to work, to free choice of employment, to just and favorable conditions of work and to protection against unemployment; (2) Everyone, without any discrimination, has the right to equal pay for equal work; (3) Everyone who works has the right to just and favorable remuneration ensuring for himself and his family an existence worthy of human dignity, and supplemented, if necessary, by other means of social protection; (4) Everyone has the right to form and to join trade unions for the protection of his interests.

First, the U.S. may be in violation because it denies incarcerated persons the opportunity of income producing work. The combination of Federal and state laws, along with a pervasive culture of exclusion almost totally excludes U.S. jail and prison inmates from participating in the U.S. jobholding economy.

Law primarily prohibits trade in inmate-produced goods. Under the Federal Sumners-Ashurst Act of 1948 (18 USC 1761) the United States by law explicitly prohibits goods produced by incarcerated persons being traded in interstate commerce. Although trade in services and intra (within) state commerce are not explicitly prohibited by U.S. Federal law, state laws and the overwhelming weight of custom effectively prohibit virtually all participation by inmates in open-market jobs.

As a result, less than 0.2 percent of America's inmates, fewer than 3,000 of almost 2 million, held open market jobs paying minimum wages or more. Of approximately 2 million U.S. inmates, it is estimated that about two-thirds lack any work assignment whatsoever; the remaining third are estimated to receive less than $1000 per year for their work, legally considered a gratuity rather than wages, and not protected under the

Fair Labor Standards Act (minimum wage protections) and without Social Security, retirement, or health benefits.[1]

Second, the United States may be in even more egregious violation of the *International Covenant on Economic, Social and Cultural Rights* because its laws and customs effectively impoverish the nation's children and families.

The consequence of the United States' prohibition on inmate employment is that, in addition to 2 million U.S. prison inmates unemployed altogether or drastically under-employed, the U.S. prohibition leaves an estimated 2.3 million minor children of U.S. jail and prison inmates unsupported by a primary caregiver.[2] About 3 percent of all U.S. children younger than 18 have an incarcerated parent; available data suggest that more than 10 percent of U.S. Black children have at least one incarcerated parent.[3] Available evidence suggests that minor children of U.S. inmates are extraordinarily likely to be in poverty. Data for Maryland indicate that on any given day 12 percent of all children receiving welfare (Temporary Assistance for Needy Families, TANF) have at least one parent incarcerated.[4] Experienced staff in the District of Columbia believe about 50 percent of D.C.'s TANF children have at least one parent who either is or was incarcerated.[5] Compounding the difficulty, the absence of a primary caregiver shifts both the financial and child care burdens to the remaining householder, most often the mother, or grandmother of the inmates' children. About 1 million – mostly low income – single householders struggle to meet family financial needs and meet the other needs of U.S. families splintered by incarceration and unemployment during incarceration; these householders meet their own needs, provide limited funds to the incarcerated family member, struggle to maintain contact with inmate family members through additional costs of telephone contact and travel for visits, all while meeting family expenses.

United States violations with respect to children and families are particularly egregious, especially in its persistent blindness to the presence of children and families and to the consequences for them. *Covenant* violations include:

In addition to *Article 7*, recognizing everyone's right to "a decent living for themselves and their families," *Article 10* emphasizes that "...The widest possible protection...should be accorded to the family...particularly for its establishment and

---

[1] American Bar Association Subcommittee on Correctional Industries, *Inmate Labor in America's Correctional Facilities*, May, 1998, pages 5 and 12, adjusted to populations for 2000.

[2] Derived from U.S. Department of Justice, Bureau of Justice Statistics Special Report, *Incarcerated Parents and Their Children,* NCJ 182335, August, 2000 to include estimates for children of jail inmates as well as of state and Federal inmates.

[3] Derived from *Incarcerated Parents and Their Children,* page 2, to account for children of jail inmates.

[4] Personal Communication, Maryland Child Support Enforcement Administration, February 11, 2000, with Thomas Petersik, "Summary of TCA Cases with Incarcerated Non-Custodial Parents, December, 1999." County percentages range from 10 to 45, averaging 12 percent statewide.

[5] Personal communication, Kate Jessburgh, District of Columbia Office of Child Support Enforcement with Thomas Petersik, 2000.

while it is responsible for the care and education of dependent children," that "special protection should be accorded to mothers during a reasonable period before and after childbirth," and "special measures of protection and assistance should be taken on behalf of all children and young persons without any discrimination for reasons of parentage or other conditions."

Recognizing that offenders are disproportionately relatively young and that their families and children are disproportionately very young, and that increasing numbers of offenders are themselves young mothers – the U.S. prison and inmate unemployment systems wreak particular havoc on the rights and special protections needed for young children and the parents of young children.

Third, potential U.S. violations extend to the terms under which inmates have access to employment:

Wages and Hours: *Article 7*, "...the right of everyone to ...fair wages and equal remuneration for work of equal value without distinction of any kind..," "...opportunity for everyone to be promoted in his employment...subject to no considerations other than those of seniority and competence," and *Article 11*, "...recognize the right of everyone to an adequate standard of living for himself and his family, including adequate food, clothing and housing..."

Health and Safety: By excluding inmates from coverage under the Fair Labor Standards Act, the inmate is also thereby effectively denied investment in the U.S. Medicare system.

Security: By excluding inmates from coverage under the Fair Labor Standards Act, the inmate is thereby effectively denied investment in the U.S. Social Security system. Recent denials of Social Security disability payments to incarcerants has the effect of impoverishing inmate families. Probable violation of *Article 9*, "The States Parties to the present Covenant recognize the right of everyone to social security, including social insurance."

Education: Through denials of higher education and training, denial of access to higher education and training, including but not limited to denial of financial support for higher education, the United States is probably in violation of the *Covenant* for educational opportunity, including violation of *Article 6*, "...will take appropriate steps to safeguard this right...[to] technical and vocational guidance and training."

Union Membership: Finally, at all levels, including the United States' current efforts allowing inmates open market jobs, the United States almost certainly violates the *Covenant's* strong stand for all worker rights to organize and belong to trade unions, particularly *Article 8*, "The right of everyone to form trade unions and to join the trade union of his choice...for the ... protection of his interests. No restrictions may be placed on the exercise of this right other than those prescribed by law and which are necessary in a democratic society in interests of national security or public order or for the protection of the rights and freedom of others," and "The right to strike, provided that it is exercised in conformity with the laws of the particular country."

V . 3 INMATES AND THE COVENANT ON ECONOMIC, SOCIAL AND CULTURAL RIGHTS

Burt Galaway, Colorado Forum on Community and Restorative Justice, USA

In summary, the *International Covenant on Economic, Social, and Cultural Rights* calls for governments to safeguard these rights:

- Self determination meaning "....the right [to] determine...political status and freely pursue....economic, social and cultural development." (Part I, *Article1*).

- The right to work "...which includes the right of everyone to the opportunity to gain his living by work which he freely chooses and accepts...." (Part III, *Article 6*).
- Social security including social insurance (Part III, *Article 9*).
- The highest attainable standard of physical and mental health (Part III, *Article 12*).
- Right of everyone to primary and secondary education and "higher education shall be made equally accessible to all, on the basis of capacity..." (Part III, *Article 13*).
- To take part in cultural life (Part III, *Article 15*).
- Medical services and medical attention.

But do these rights apply to inmates? Should prison administrators be held accountable for assuring these rights to inmates? Arguing that, by default, they apply to inmates since the *Covenant* does not explicitly provide an exception for inmates is a weak argument especially in the light of Part II, *Article 4* that provides for limitations on the rights "... for the purpose of promoting the general welfare in a democratic society."

Starting with a position about the purpose of prisons can provide a stronger line of argument for making these rights available to inmates. One must take into consideration two indisputable facts while thinking about the purpose of prisons. First, practically all inmates are released back to society—very few die in prison. Second, prisons are very expensive and require huge amounts of money that is not, therefore, available for other social purposes. What then can citizens reasonably expect from their prisons? What is a reasonable return for their investment?

Minimally citizens should be able to expect that inmates released from prison should be better equipped to function in a democratic society than they were when admitted to prison. Is the investment in prisons worthwhile unless the product is improved ability to function in society? The rights stated in the *Covenant* suggest criteria to use for evaluating the return being received on citizen investment in prisons.

- Does the prison experience prepare inmates for self-determination? Are inmates at release better about making decisions than they were at admission?
- Has the inmate been working and improving work skills and habits while incarcerated? Is he/she a more skillful worker with improved work habits at release than when he/she was admitted?

Have the same social security benefits been extended to the inmate while in prison that are extended to persons in the community? Does the inmate continue paying into trust funds so that eligibility for future benefits is not compromised?

- Have the physical and mental health of the inmate been protected, so that he/she leaves prison mentally and physically healthier than when admitted?
- Has the inmate's educational level improved consistent with his/her capacity?
- Has the inmate participated in cultural activities similar to those available to all citizens and is he/she committed to continue participation in the cultural life of the community?

There is no systematic reporting of the extent to which inmates leave American prisons better able to function in a democratic society than when they were admitted. One can probably safely speculate, however, that most American prisons would receive a failing grade if evaluated against criteria derived from the *Covenant*.

A system of accountability is needed to hold prison administrators responsible for making a decent return on the investment they receive from citizens. I suggest two modest steps toward prison accountability:

- Prison administrators should be required to make annual reports to the public and to their funding bodies about the steps they have taken to comply with the *Covenant* and thus strengthen the skills of inmates for living in a democratic society.
- Research about prison effectiveness should focus specifically on the extent to which inmates at discharge have improved their skills to live in a democratic society.

V . 4 STALLED HUMAN RIGHTS

Rachel Stafford, U.S. Offenders Litigation Program, London, England

Human Rights ... an emotive subject ... and again ... words. It is not words we need but ACTION. The history of your country's legal system is, without doubt, a relic of our pre-independence influence, and, I have to say, it gives me great shame. We started to debate the subject of Human Rights post World War II in the light of the Holocaust atrocities. At the end of the day, we look at impressive words on paper.

1997, the convention concerning the abolition of forced labor. Look at the structure of pay for the prisoners in your own country. I refer you to the Wall Street Journal, Thursday, March 15, 2001, "Prison As A Profit Center." For example, the Oregon Department of Corrections expects that by 2006 it will make ten million dollars a year from its inmates, but what for the inmate? And what about rehabilitation? We fall behind our European cousins.

Ideas do not alter, words become more elaborate, but we do not effect any real change. Let's move forward and use, not words, but action. In 1955 came the promulgation of the U.N. Standard Minimum Rule for Treatment of Prisoners but, again, we are no further forward, just an elaborate form of window dressing.

V . 5 HOLDING PRISONS ACCOUNTABLE FOR HEALTH CARE

Carol Martindale-Taylor, Maryland, USA

§12.2.d of the International Covenant on Economic, Social and Cultural Rights states that States will achieve "The creation of conditions which would assure to all medical service and medical attention in the event of sickness."

I want to share with you some of the problems and frustrations felt by inmates and their families in dealing with the health care systems in prison. My husband is an HIV+ inmate and is under "chronic care" in a large, maximum-security level institution. Let me give you some examples of the health care problems he has had over the years.

1. After being seen for an infected tooth - it took 4 days for the dental tech to check him - he was advised it would be pulled when the dentist was on site (a few days away). To "hold him over", he was given an antibiotic which resulted in an allergic reaction causing him to develop hives. After the repeated submission of sick call slips, he was seen 5 days later - and was covered with hives from his lower jaw to his knees. He was then given medication for the hives (and a different antibiotic) that proved ineffective for controlling the hives. My husband filed a grievance over this incident, which was never addressed. I called the medical director at the facility, who apologized and asked that I send it directly to him. He never responded to this second attempt. If you ask about remedies in this kind of situation, you are told to "take it to court". Needless to say, that is something that most inmates cannot do, especially those who have no money and no family to help in the process.

2. My husband was told he needed minor surgery and the doctor recommended he be taken to a local hospital. One year later, the same doctor made the same recommendation - and my husband had been submitting sick call slips during the interim.

3. It took one year for a medical slip on a foot problem to be handled.

4. As many of you may know, HIV medications require strict adherence to guidelines such as taking one medication on an empty stomach and another with food. The facility where my husband is incarcerated instituted a "watch-take" system, meaning that the inmate has to be observed physically swallowing the medications. This also means that two drugs with conflicting diet regimes have to be taken simultaneously. During the two different time frames when this policy was in place, he developed severe diarrhea, lost weight, and ultimately suffered a rebound in his viral load.

5. Approximately two years ago, some young inmates were apparently concerned about something my husband had witnessed. As a result, he was later trapped in the dorm shower, stabbed multiple times, puncturing one lung, and received 1st, 2nd, and 3rd degree burns on the side of his face, neck, and chest from heated baby oil being thrown on him. After four days in a university hospital, he was transferred to the prison infirmary, with his outside physician taking care to prescribe pain medication for him. He then spent two days with absolutely no pain medication in the prison hospital. When he asked for it, the staff said they would "check on it", but no one ever returned. Upon investigating, the CO was able to obtain Tylenol

(the physician's prescription had expired!), and to have his bedding changed as it was covered with dead skin that had been sloughing off.

6. Recently, he suffered a deep laceration above his eye while involved in a basketball game. When he reported to the infirmary, the nurse just told him to take an aspirin and that it did not appear to require stitches. He had to re-open the wound to show her how long and deep it was!

7. Another incident occurred when he had typical symptoms related to passing kidney stones. Although one of his HIV medications is known for causing kidney stones, it was not diagnosed as such until his second attack. When he experienced the first attack late in the evening, another inmate called to let me know that my husband was in severe pain and awaiting transport to the medical unit. I called the facility at 10:50 p.m. to check on his condition, and was informed by a CO that it wouldn't do any good to try to reach anyone in the medical unit as they get off work at 11:00 p.m. and there's no one there again until 7:00 a.m. When I asked "Are you telling me that he could die in there over night and I wouldn't know it?" His response was "Yes, that is a possibility."

Dealing with these incidents has taken many certified letters (and always get a signature showing that your correspondence has been received!) and many telephone calls. I have been in contact with medical directors, wardens, assistant wardens, the Commissioner's office, the national headquarters of private health care providers, correctional officers, and even people in state government responsible for contracting with the providers. All you can do is hope that the inmate isn't suffering, and that he or she survives whatever illness or accident has occurred.

I wish I could say my husband's case is the exception. Unfortunately, I cannot - I can list numerous other such instances in his facility. Professional training for all staff would go a long way to fix this problem; however, as I mentioned earlier, without adequate support, the medical staff will never be able to function professionally. Additionally, those individuals who are professional and do care about the quality of health care, are not going to survive working in such an atmosphere. In fact, I know of at least two such people who resigned for this very reason.

Citing violations to the various Conventions is a theme that I have been hearing the last few days, and as others have suggested, I too believe this would give credibility to both our cause and to the Conventions themselves.

V . 6 EXCERPTS FROM THE CONFERENCE REPORT CARDS

FOR BRAZIL: The grievance procedures are rarely effective. Prisoners are afraid to denounce injustice for fear of reprisals.

FOR FRANCE: Children cannot visit their imprisoned relatives at a satisfying frequency as prisons are most of the time hundreds of kms. away from the place of residence.

Chapter VI.
Prison is Torture:
Convention Against Torture and Covenant on Civil and Political Rights

§2.1 of the Convention Against Torture and Other Cruel, Inhuman or Degrading Treatment or Punishment states that "Each State Party shall take effective legislative, administrative, judicial or other measures to prevent acts of torture in any territory under its jurisdiction."
§16 of the Convention against Torture and Other Cruel, Inhuman or Degrading Treatment or Punishment states that "Each State Party shall undertake to prevent in any territory under its jurisdiction other acts of cruel, inhuman or degrading treatment or punishment which do not amount to torture... when such acts are committed by or at the instigation of or with the consent of or acquiescence of a public official or other person acting in an official capacity."
§7 of the Covenant on Civil and Political Rights states that "No one shall be subjected to torture or to cruel, inhuman or degrading treatment or punishment."
§10.1 of the Covenant on Civil and Political Rights states that, "All persons deprived of their liberty shall be treated with humanity and with respect for the inherent dignity of the human person."

VI . 1 Do Control or Super Max Prisons and Other Punitive Punishments Violate The Document on Torture?

Bonnie Kerness, Assoc. Director AFSC Criminal Justice Program, Coordinator, Prisonwatch, New Jersey, USA

Mass incarceration has brought profound - and profoundly disturbing - changes in the very nature of imprisonment. Most prominent among these is the escalating use of isolation through control units and supermax prisons.

I've been a human rights advocate on behalf of prisoners for the American Friends Service Committee for over 25 years. Because I've watched the development of the use of extended isolation for the past two and a half decades, I'd like to share some of my observations on the evolution. Studies of the recent history of incarceration suggest that isolation and sensory deprivation were initially used in the late 1960's as a technique for behavior modification with prisoners involved in the prisoners' rights movement, Islamic militants, jailhouse lawyers and ethnically based prison gangs. It soon became clear that isolation was used for a select group of prisoners including activists jailed as a result of the Counterintelligence Program of the FBI for both nonviolent and violent political actions. These groups all posed challenges to the balance of power inside prisons. The concerns raised by these groups about racism, brutality, overcrowding and so on garnered considerable visibility and support from outside prison walls, with a notable impact on broad segments of community opinion and, ultimately, a measure of vindication in the courts.

As with other social movements, the prisoners' rights movement and its outside support waned by the end of the 1970's. But control units, once established, became an increasingly normalized part of the prison environment and began to proliferate throughout the system. Today, supermax prisons are seen as a cost effective way of managing the huge increases in the incarcerated population: a labor saving measure that permits large numbers of prisoners to be controlled by fewer officers.

In 1997, the U.S. Department of Justice conducted a survey of supermax housing and found there to be 57 supermax facilities or units nationwide with ten Departments of Correction pursuing the development of 3,000 additional supermax beds. In responding to the query on the factors involved in the development of supermax housing, DOCS noted, among other things, legislative interest and the availability of federal Crime Bill construction funds.

DOCS also mentioned the need to better manage gang activists as a factor in the development of supermax facilities. There is another 1997 Department of Justice national survey which was administered to DOCS throughout the country. This one centered on "Security Threat Groups" in prisons and asked Departments to list their 10 most disruptive gangs. The results of this state-by-state survey are revealing. The State of Kentucky notes that the Aryan Brotherhood is adversarial with all Black groups, which is not true. Minnesota and Oregon simply named Asians as "gangs", which Minnesota further compounds by adding "Native Americans" as gangs. The State of New Jersey lists the Black Cat Collective as a gang. The Black Cat Collective is my free foster son who, along with three of his friends, put on Afro-centric cultural programs at libraries. The very definition of what constitutes a gang merits questioning.

Corrections personnel have also told me that the nation-wide move to expand the use of isolation in supermax prisons is being fostered by correctional officer unions with unions contributing heavily to the political campaigns of law and order candidates.

These past years for me have been full of thousands of calls and complaints of an increasingly disturbing nature. I hear from people locked in supermax prisons throughout the country, and there are similarities to their complaints. Many describe cold, filth, callous medical care, extended isolation sometimes lasting well over a decade, use of devices of torture, harassment, brutality, and racism. I have received vivid descriptions of four point restraints, restraint hoods, restraint beds, restraint belts, stun grenades, stun guns, stun belts, tethers, and waist and leg chains. Family members report that during visits their prisoner relatives remained standing, shackled and chained to poles despite the thick Plexiglas between visitors and their prisoner loved ones. I've had reports of visits only being allowed via a small video screen. In other cases, prisoners tell me of being strip searched for a window visit, including a humiliating anal probe. This, despite the fact that they've had no human contact for months and will have none during the visit. I continue to monitor people who have been held in isolation for the past fifteen to twenty years.

The AFSC has received so much credible testimony, including drawings, that we have produced two pamphlets. The first is a "Survivor's Manual" written by prisoners living in extended isolation, for prisoners living in extended isolation. The second is a pamphlet of testimonies of torture from isolation units and prisons all over the country.

Many aspects of the conditions in U.S. control units and supermax facilities violate international United Nations Covenants and Treaties to which the U.S. is a signatory. The UN Human Rights Committee stated in 1995 that conditions in certain US maximum security prisons were incompatible with international standards. The UN Special Rapporteur on Torture reported in 1996 on cruel, inhuman, and degrading treatment in several U.S. supermax prisons. And in 2000, the UN Committee on Torture cited the U.S. for what they called the "widespread" use of devices of torture in U.S. prisons.

In the mid-nineties, I began working with the World Organization Against Torture on two reports detailing U.S. compliance with the *Convention Against Torture and the Convention on the Elimination of All Forms of Racial Discrimination.* The type of conditions and treatment in control units or supermax prisons was cited in these reports as crossing the line involving inhuman and abusive punishment prohibited under these *UN Conventions*. The Report on compliance with the *Convention Against Torture* found that there were a number of criminal justice policies and practices that "constitute cruel, inhuman, or degrading punishment" of the type prohibited under *Article 1* of the *Convention Against Torture*, and under other numerous legally binding international human rights instruments. Among the areas named where the U.S. government was not meeting its obligations to prevent highly abusive conduct were "the use of punitive violence and brutality in specially created super-maximum and control unit facilities; indefinite and arbitrary solitary confinement, the practice of punitive 'cell extractions' and the treatment of the mentally ill in prisons."

The conditions that men and women endure in U.S. prisons also violate the *UN International Covenant on Civil and Political Rights*, the *UN Standard Minimum Rules for the Treatment of Prisoners* and, in some cases, even the approved practices of the American Correctional Association. We have found that mentally ill and mentally retarded prisoners continue to be assigned to some supermax facilities despite evidence that the conditions are particularly damaging and inappropriate for them. Other prisoners develop mental illness while in the units. We have also found in numerous cases segregation being used as a form of retribution.

AFSC believes that isolation units, supermax prisons, sensory deprivation, brutality toward prisoners and the use of devices of torture are all violations, not only of human rights, but also of fundamental decency. All have little or nothing to do with the safe and orderly operation of correctional institutions - and everything to do with the spread of a culture of violence and dehumanization. With each passing year, such practices have become more routinized throughout the prison system. These measures are beginning to spread to county jails, juvenile facilities, and prisons for women. In these times particularly, there is a pressing need to safeguard the legacy of civil rights in the U.S. and to demand at least the minimum human rights protection enshrined in international human rights standards.

The culture of violence is profoundly destructive to those who suffer its effects, brutalizing not only prisoners, but also correctional officers and officials who become the daily agents of inhumanity. The larger community is also gravely harmed - not only by the practical difficulties of reintegrating human beings who have been so deeply traumatized, but also by the profound erosion of our simple humanity.

VI . 2 THE DIGNITY OF THE PERSON AS IT APPLIES TO SUPERMAX PRISONS

Mason Nottingham, Virginia-CURE, Virginia, USA

Supermaxes in Virginia

We have two supermax prisons in Virginia. My impression is that the words supermax were a formidable fad in the corrections establishment, and it was in a context involving two things which are also a national trend. They are: (1) have a hierarchy of prisons where the worst of the worst are in separate institutions from others, and (2) the whole prison establishment would be intimidated by the threat of supermaxes. Each objective was to create a safer prison system for both staff and prisoners. As far as we can tell the system is a little safer now as measured by fewer lockdowns and slightly less assault of prisoners on staff and each other. The degree of assault of staff on prisoner is as everywhere an unknown statistic. What is clear is that we in Virginia have a case of overkill arising from political bravado and over zealousness of the black hat image which seems to usually have an upper hand in corrections in the U.S.

We of course favor no supermaxes at all given the definition of 23 hour lockdown for a minimum of two years. If you have one, though, a system of our size and make-up would warrant no more that 200 or so cells, not the arbitrary, see how tough we are, level of 800. Further, we have a dire need of independent and hard nosed oversight of the use of supermaxes and overuse of stun guns, four point restraints, pellet guns and other implements.

Early UN struggle about what rights are about

Do we respect man? By this I mean every person. Does our dignity or worth not demand that we do so? The struggles of the UN since inception are a help for us - we who think of ourselves as a hotbed of rights, given our Constitution and our Virginia heritage. We and nations of all sorts are joined in a determination to promote persons as having a dignity accompanied with rights and responsibilities for each other.

A book which Charlie Sullivan recommended to us is *A World Made New - Eleanor Roosevelt and the Universal Declaration of Human Rights* by Mary Ann Glendon. This and the *Human Rights for All* booklet which C.E. Cypser compiled for us are enormous resources for us all to digest and cull from quite beyond preparation for our few days here. It is with great pride that I learn, from the book, that what we are engaged in here first of all is a *Declaration of Rights* which came out of a struggle early in the formation of the United Nations and that the leader was our beloved Eleanor Roosevelt, wife of our president Franklin Delano Roosevelt. Since it is not binding law, then we are called to see what is engraved in our hearts just as it is a guide for subsequent international law.

I want to offer the following for each of us, of whatever faith or none, hoping it will unite us further in the concept of the dignity or sacredness of the human. It is a quote from a French philosopher/theologian of very high stature: "... the deepest layer of the human person's dignity consists in its property of resembling God ... It is in the image of God. For God is spirit and the human person proceeds from Him in having as principle of life a spiritual soul capable of knowing, loving and of being uplifted by grace to participation in the very life of God so that in the end, it might know and love Him as He knows and loves Himself." (*The Person and the Common Good;* Jacques Maritain; paperback; University of Notre Dame Press; p.42.)

We are called by that statement to consider ourselves and every "human person" as resembling God because we are in his image due to our spiritual nature. If you doubt there is a God, then accept that man and woman possess good inner forces of both love and dignity and that this force is the greater force, the one we are called to promote. We have only words to pass on our inner knowledge and the best universal pair of words to explain human dignity, in my view, are "spiritual soul," an expression which should be suitable to all religious or non religious alike. Neglect of our spiritual soul invites lethargy, our greatest sin, and permits torture and other abuse. It enables us to think in terms of the other as if we have no responsibility. Is torture or anything like it bearable amongst us?

The climate in Virginia has become improved and there is some hope for us. I have roughly drafted the following omnibus bill reflecting the concerns of this convention.

Whereas Virginia has a relatively peaceful prison population, we must turn from inordinate punitive treatment of the so-called worst of the worst. This includes conversion of our level 6 supermax prisons and level 5 prisons to more humane purposes and practices.

Whereas Virginia's resort to use of force implements has exceeded other states and our prison population is relatively peaceful, we must withdraw extensive use of use of force implements except where demonstrably needed. Further, written reporting and review of every such use must be required. Details should be summarized and made available in regular summary form for General Assembly and public review.

Whereas public trust in the humane and effective care of prisoners is required for a Virginia people insistent on living in the highest level of human dignity, a board, independent of the executive branch and consisting of private citizens, independent of professional corrections experts and legislators, must be mandated and supported by an adequate staff in their employ. The board and its staff should have a mandate of investigating and reporting on prison practices according to accepted standards with full authority to perform oversight such as now residing in the distant and under-funded responsibility of the Federal Department of Civil Rights. They would be specifically charged with review of use of force implements, criteria, and practice in use of segregation cells especially for prolonged periods, establishing a cap on the number of persons in prolonged confinement.

Whereas Federal and State constitutional constraints are said to condone current practice in Virginia it is incumbent for the General Assembly to enact explicit standards and understandings for upholding the dignity of its population as it pertains to the imprisoned. All persons are born free and equal in human dignity and rights including felons and other prisoners and ex-prisoners. All have the right to recognition everywhere, as a person of human dignity before the law including in criminal justice. No person shall be subject to torture or cruel, inhuman or degrading treatment or punishment. (see *Universal Declaration of Human Rights* - 1, 6, 2).

VI . 3 A PRISON EXPERIENCE IN MALAWI

Dr. Vera M. Chirwa, Special Rapporteu, Prisons and Conditions of Detention in Africa

Torture has been defined as the intentional affliction of severe physical or psychological pain or suffering, for a specific purpose. It could be for making someone talk, or for the purpose of punishing him or her, or for the intention of intimidating, dehumanizing, or degrading. Torture as most used these days is a weapon against freedom and democracy. It is used to extract information or confession from a victim (e.g. in police cells) to punish, to take revenge, to intimidate or to create terror and fear in the victim, to dehumanize or degrade the victim. The aim of torture is not to kill, though we have heard of instances of victims tortured to death (police cells in SA prisons and detention centers). In short it is used to breakdown the victim's personality. Torture dehumanizes and makes the victim sub-human. Torture is a violation of one's human rights. In this paper I am concerned about torture in prisons and police cells. In these institutions we find many ways or situations, which amount to torture.

Overcrowding: If a cell is overcrowded, occupants are tortured in that their freedom of movement is restricted; also there is no freedom to fresh air or ventilation. Inmates are subjected to an unhygienic environment and suffer from diseases; for example, scabs, TB, and other contagious diseases. Assaults, abusive language, denial of food, medicine, visits, clean water, soap, beddings, and the like is torture. In short, denial of a person's basic inborn rights amounts to torture. Assault and beating up of prisoners are more obvious forms of torture.

I myself was a prisoner for 12 years (1981-1993). My husband, Orton Chirwa and our oldest son, Fumbani, were kidnapped in Zambia (as refugees) by Malawi security forces into Malawi where we were charged with treason and tried by a kangaroo court comprised of appointees of the President. We were convicted and incarcerated for years. We were subjected to all sorts of dehumanizing and humiliating treatment, which amounted to torture. For example, we were chained hands and feet, day in and day out, and in solitary confinement. A bucket was used as a toilet during the night and day. The same bucket was used as a bath after emptying it in the morning. We slept on the cement floor. The food was bad, unpalatable, and sometimes rotten. I was continually humiliated in front of guards and my fellow political prisoners. I felt pain in my heart, a very sharp pain; so, in prison I experienced both psychological and physical pain or torture.

The day we were sentenced to death, they removed everything from the cell, including water. We were denied food, the whole day, and in the evening they chained my hands so tightly that in the morning the chains had sunk in my flesh, tearing it, and blood appeared. My arms were very swollen. Prisons became death traps. I was lucky to survive, but my husband was murdered during the eleventh year of imprisonment by injecting him with a lethal gas injection. Our son was tortured by subjecting him to electrical shocks and using instruments on his body. He has scars all over his body; he is not the same as he was. He experienced post-traumatic stress disorders, anxiety, and social withdrawal. He sometimes spends the whole day in his bedroom, talking to no-one.

African governments presided over by first generation presidents had no political will to make prisons more humane and less demoralizing. In fact, prisons were institutions of terror and humiliation, used as a weapon for silencing opposition or any other enemy. Some governments and prisons still operate under that brutal idea.

However, this negative attitude is changing. This is shown in that heads of state and governments adopted the African Charter. This charter provides for equal protection before the law and for the inviolability of the human being, ensuring the right to life and personal integrity. It affirms that the inherent integrity of a human being should be respected and that the human being should not be subjected to cruel, inhuman, or degrading punishment.

In order for heads of state to see that human rights are generally promoted and protected in Africa, they put in place an institution called the African Commission on Individual and Peoples' Rights which has nominated a Special Rapporteur on Prisons in Africa among its members. The Special Rapporteur is to specifically give attention to prisons and prisoners' rights. The Special Rapporteur's job is to visit prisons in Africa, inspect conditions of prisons, and make specific recommendations with a view to improving the prisons.

VI . 4 TORTURE AND PRISON ABOLITION

Antonio Pedro Dores, President of Assoc. Contra a Excluso pelo Desenvolvimento, (Portugal)

In Portugal we have some of the finest laws, from the humanistic point of view, for treatment and rehabilitation of the convicted. We have the lowest rate of crime in Europe. But, at the same time, we have the largest rate of inmates, the largest rate of inmates dying in prison, and the largest rate of ill inmates. In brief: good prison reform laws do not mean better lives for those in prison.

We can conclude, from experience we all have in each country, that there is no prison without Human Rights violations. So, the conclusion should be: Stop the imprisonment!

Prison is meant to be a torture. We, so called civilized people, used to explain to our selves that it is "only" a psychological torture. We say that only by mistake sometimes, due to the tension, that physical torture also happens and should be punished. But every activist knows that it is not like that: physical torture comes with the prison system; and, even it could be not so, psychological torture only can be separated from physical torture in an analytical way, i.e. as an abstract analysis. Prison is always a torture, whether we like it or not.

To conceive theoretically of a society without prison is not to present a new society. It is to join the struggle for better justice - for restorative justice even though we do not really know yet how it would work in a society where it would have priority over punitive justice.

The humanistic development of the world should restrict the use of prison systems. Fewer inmates is, of course, a sign of better justice and of quiet and productive lives for more people. From this aggregate point of view too, the stoppage of prison usage would be a logical way to progress for human kind.

The money and human resources expended in prison systems is contrary to humanity's interests. We should install a supportive network of concepts and people to push forward the belief that prisons are not humane institutions. That is our collective task for the generations to come.

VI . 5 EXCERPTS FROM THE CONFERENCE REPORT CARDS

FOR FRANCE: The European Committee on the Prevention of Torture stated that detention conditions in Marseilles and Paris amounted to cruel, inhuman and degrading treatment.

As prisons are overcrowded, there is a high rate of rapes by inmates. Because of the lack of prison personnel, nothing is done to insure the security of prisoners.

FOR PERU: As there is no proper control of the prison authorities, it is difficult to prosecute cases.

FOR BRAZIL: Torture continues with impunity. Denouncements are met with bureaucratic blocks. People are afraid to denounce for fear of more torture.

FOR USA: The cruel use of restraint devices, pepper spray, and electro-shock stun-belts are all too common, resulting in unnecessary pain or injury.

More and more prisoners are being confined in Control-Unit prisons or so-called Special Housing Units where they have 23-hour lockdowns, limited human contact, limited exercise, and limited stimulation. Prisoners have been confined in these units for months and years, and prolonged isolation can cause severe physical and psychological damage. Mentally ill prisoners are more likely than other inmates to end up in such units because of behavioral difficulties in prison, and lack of resources to treat them. Other prisoners develop mental illness while in the unit.[1] Prison staff are often poorly trained and generally poorly supervised, leading to emotional and, occasionally, physical abuses.

Excessive punishments have resulted from the widespread use of mandatory minimums, which deprive judges of judicial discretion. America's overly harsh drug laws have resulted in unnecessary confinement of tens of thousands of low-level, non-violent offenders. These imprisonments are disproportionately severe punishments.

---

[1] *United States of America, Rights for All*, Amnesty International, NY, 1998, p. 77.

Chapter VII.
Rights of Women in Prison; Convention on Women Covenant on Civil and Political Rights

§10.1 of the Covenant on Civil and Political Rights states that, "All persons deprived of their liberty shall be treated with humanity and with respect for the inherent dignity of the human person."

§12 of the Convention on the Elimination of All Forms of Discrimination against Women requires that "States Parties shall ensure to women appropriate services in connection with pregnancy, confinement and the post-natal period, granting free services where necessary, as well as adequate nutrition during pregnancy and lactation."

VII . 1 THE MISTREATMENT OF WOMEN

Heidi Cernaka, Prison Pastoral in Brazil, Women Inmate Ministry, Brazil

Female inmates in Brazil are forgotten by all. In the state of São Paulo, which houses half of the inmates in the entire country, women make up about 6% of all of the prisoners. Because they are fewer and incite fewer rebellions, their cry for justice, or rather, a more humane situation is heard by practically no one.

1. Profile of Women Prisoners in Sao Paulo

The prison census in August of 2001 counted 5157 women in jails and prisons in São Paulo. In a study done in the Women's penitentiary in Tatuapé in 1997, 75% of the women were working before being imprisoned. According to the Inter-Syndicate Department of Statistics and Socio-Economic Studies (DIEESE), 44.2% of women are in the informal economy- this most often refers to work as a housekeeper or to work selling merchandise on sidewalks and in the streets, vulnerable to the changing economy and with absolutely no benefits or legal recourse. 86.5% of them have underage children of which 78% are now living with the inmate's parents. 78% of them had extremely low incomes and 50% have never completed primary school. 81% of them were between 21-40 years of age. And 50% are not in jail for the first time- which also shows the "inefficiency of the system in the reintegration of the woman prisoner into society." Almost 20% passed through the state facilities for minors, either as young offenders or children who had nowhere else to live.

2. Health Problems

The two public women's jails in Pinheiros (known as Dacar 1 and 4) do not even have minimal hygienic conditions. Until two years ago, they did not have electricity in the cells, in other words, no lights and no outlets. The women are locked in their cells from 5PM until 9AM the next day. Each jail has a maximum capacity of 512 women, and they currently house more than 700 women each. The inmates receive neither mattresses nor blankets. Their families or visitors, if they have them, have to supply all of their basic necessities. If her family cannot afford the bus fare, lives far away, or if she has no visitors, a woman suffers from the cold and often ends up sick. In the winter, the temperature can get into the 40's (7-8°C) at night. They do not receive soap, toilet paper or sanitary napkins. Seeing as the majority are still young enough to menstruate, this is not only a lack of hygiene, but also a serious public health problem.

The health of a woman inmate is ignored. Not only in the public jails, but even in the Penitentiary in Tatuapé, medicines as well as dental and medical staff is lacking. A pap smear is a virtually unheard of event. As far as women who are pregnant, HIV+ or have tuberculosis, medical accompaniment is practically nonexistent. The two public jails and the women's penitentiary have infirmaries equipped for basic medical service, but they have no physician to staff them. For any medical need, they have to take the prisoner either to the emergency room, the nearest public health clinic, or to a penitentiary that has ambulatory services. This complicates the situation for many reasons. To take an inmate anywhere, first, the staff must be willing. In addition, there needs to be enough staff "leftover" that can leave to accompany and guard the inmate, and a vehicle that is functioning (not always the case). In one of the two public jails, the head jailer said that each shift carries between 12- 20 women out for medical care. The SSP does not have enough people to do this regularly, and therefore, the women end up not going. A regular shift has between 6-7 guards for 700 women.

The Federal Constitution of Brazil guarantees the inmate's right to breastfeed a newborn child for 4-6 months. In the three years that the Prison Pastoral has been present in Dacar, few of the more than 100 pregnant inmates have been able to breastfeed. A lack of a bed and crib in the wing of the prison set up for pregnant women and a lack of staff are the most often cited reasons for denying women the right to breastfeed. Because of this failure of the system, both the mother and her child are negatively affected. For more than a year, the maternity wing of the prison hospital was ready to open- with beds, medical materials and cribs. It stayed closed because of a lack of staff, and because of this lack of staff and guards, dozens and dozens of women gave birth and were forced to return to their cells within 24 hours, still bleeding and with breasts heavy with milk. If they have family, someone has to pick up the child and raise it in the mother's place. If they do not have family, the child must go to an institution, at times to be lost in the system because he/she does not have a birth certificate, and at times, to disappear into the adoption world, generally against the will and without the authorization of the mother.

One woman pregnant with twins at the penitentiary asked for medical assistance on a Sunday, because she was feeling pain. On Wednesday, the doctor looked at her, diagnosed a urinary tract infection and medicated her. On Thursday, she was finally taken to the emergency room, already in labor and delivered one baby already dead and another that died within 12 hours. This is not only a lack of medical assistance, but also a crime, for which the State also is guilty for not providing adequate prenatal care.

3. The Judiciary Situation

The number of women entering into the prison system grows daily, increasing the proportion of women to men overall. No structure or plan exists to accompany this growth. The majority of the women are imprisoned in the two public jails in Pinheiros.

These jails were not built for women, and offer no means to meet any basic needs of theirs. In Brazil, for every three days worked, an inmate earns one day of remission, meaning one day off his/her sentence. Without work, there is no remission. The majority end up completing their entire sentence in the public jail, with no chance to work, earn remission or take literacy courses. The women that are sentenced to "semi-open" prison (can leave during the day to work, but must return by 7PM), or have earned the right to progression of their sentence (from closed jail to semi-open), or have earned the right to parole which means she could be home caring for her children, stay in jail due to the absolute slowness of the judiciary system.

4. Torture

Torture still exists in the jails in São Paulo. Few have the courage to denounce torture, because they know they will pay a high price for opening their mouths. Psychological torture also exists, when jailers or military police enter in the cells at night, shooting over the women's heads, shouting and threatening them. Some torture has been denounced. In one jail, the women complained that when they ask to see the doctor, they are taken from their cells to the infirmary. Waiting in line for the doctor, the head guard beats them, with the objective of trying to get them to stop asking to see the doctor. Two women signed denouncements in December of 2000, and gave testimony before a judge of all that they had suffered. 6 months later, they are still in the same jail, suffering death threats and threats of more torture. How can one motivate people to denounce torture when they do not see any positive results for their risk, and even more so, are continually threatened, and lose their chances at parole because the jail gives them a negative behavioral review?

5. Visits and Conjugal Visits

The public jails are on the extreme peripheries of the city. A visit for many families involves a trip that takes hours and relies on many different means of transportation. At times, they may pay up to 6 buses and subways to get from their home to the jail and back. Beyond this, the situation of visits for women prisoners is different than for men. The mothers of the women, many times, are busy taking care of the women's children while the woman is in jail. Therefore, the mother of the female inmate has less time and less money leftover to make this trip. Certainly, the lines at the doors of the women's jail on visiting day are always much shorter than the lines to visit the men's jail. The National Council of Criminal and Penitentiary policy, through its Resolution number 1 on March 30, 1999, recommended to the State Penitentiary departments, that they guarantee to all prisoners (men and women) the right to conjugal visits at least once a month. Nowhere in the state of São Paulo do women have this right, be that for fear of pregnancies, lack of adequate space to guarantee privacy or lack of organization on the part of the prison. Conjugal visits do not happen in the women's prisons. It is blatant discrimination, seeing as the men have access to this right.

6. Drug Trafficking

While the most commonly committed crime among men is armed robbery, among women, it is drug trafficking. Only 10% of men's convictions are for drug trafficking, while 47.6% of the women's convictions are. It is clear that many women use and sell drugs to support their own addictions. However, in the majority of the cases, the women are not the big dealers, but are arrested with a few grams of drugs or a few "rocks" of crack cocaine. One woman was convicted to three years of prison for "trafficking" 21 grams of marijuana! While they are aware of what they are doing, many women sell or pass drugs either because they are desperate to take care of their children (and cannot refuse an offer of good money just to "carry drugs."), or because their boyfriend convinces them to traffic for him.

7. Conclusions

It is important to state that we know guards and staff that are trying to do their best in an impossible situation. Unfortunately, we also know guards that believe they have impunity to torture and abuse the women physically and psychologically. We know of at least one case of torture that was denounced, and the guard is being charged in a criminal court, instead of just a hearing within the police system.

The majority of the women are mothers. It is too bad that there is no type of recovery programs, educational programs or literacy in the public jails. The woman prisoner always loses out. She often loses contact with her family, or at least damages the relationship with her family, their confidence in her and practically any chance of having a job afterwards, because she has a criminal record. It is lamentable also, that alternative sentencing does not exist; those who commit nonviolent crimes should have a chance to be sentenced to home prison, semi-open prison or probation. After three years in prison, the damage to her health and to her family is many times irrecoverable.

Until we recognize that women are in the penal system and their numbers are growing, we are going to continue to leave them in inadequate and temporary spaces, ignoring their medical and judicial necessities, at the mercy of abuse of power and physical and psychological torture. Until we really enter into the "re-education" and re-socialization of prisoners and build more adequate public policies, not only will the female inmates and their children suffer the price of this injustice, but all of society too.

VII. 2 EXCERPTS FROM THE CONFERENCE REPORT CARDS

FOR BRAZIL: Unnecessary body searches on visits are severely uncomfortable and an offense to human dignity.

FOR USA: Reported sexual abuses by correctional staff include rape and other coerced sexual acts; staff routinely subjecting inmates to sexually offensive language; staff deliberately touching intimate parts of inmate's bodies during searches; and staff watching inmates who are undressed.[1] The employment of male staff to supervise female prisoners breaches international standards, which provide that male staff must not enter a prison set aside for women unless accompanied by a female officer, and that women prisoners must be attended and supervised only by women officers.

---

[1] *United States of America, Rights for All*, Amnesty International, NY, 1998, p. 62.

Chapter VIII.
Prisons Are Racist; Convention Against Racism Covenant on Civil and Political Rights

§5.a of the Convention on the Elimination of All Forms of Racial Discrimination requires, "The right to equal treatment before the tribunals and all other organs administering justice."
§14.1 of the Covenant on Civil and Political Rights states that, "All persons shall be equal before the courts and tribunals. In the determination of any criminal charge against him, everyone shall be entitled to a fair and public hearing by a competent, independent and impartial tribunal established by law."

VIII . 1 RACIAL DISPARITIES IN THE "GREAT MIGRATION" TO PRISON

Peter Wagner, Western New England College, Massachusetts, USA

No credible evidence has been introduced that raising the New York State prison population from 12,579 in 1970 to 71,466 in 2000 has made a change in the rate that crime occurs. Despite having more police per capita than another other state, and despite spending $1 billion a year to operate prisons, New York faces approximately the same degree of crime it has faced since the start of crime statistics in the 1930s.

What New York has done in recent decades is incarcerate an increasing number of its Black, Latino and Indigenous citizens. Minorities account for 87.6% of the growth in New York's prison population since 1970. Within the shorter period of 1985 - 1997, the figure was 90%, higher than any other state.

Since 1930, the odds of being sent to prison in New York State for a White person in a given year has actually fallen slightly, but the odds of a Black person being sent to prison in a given year has risen more than 250%. In 1930, the Black-White disparity in prison commitment rates was offensive at 4.1 times higher for Blacks. In 2000, that disparity has risen to the level of a democratic calamity with Blacks being 11.1 times more likely to be sent to prison in a given year than Whites.

Ninety seven out of every 100,000 White New Yorkers is currently in prison. For Latinos, it's 776, and for Blacks the figure is 1,295 per 100,000. That's a Black-White disparity of 13.4 times.

In one 1994 study of court biases, it found that more than a quarter of the imprisonment of Blacks in New York could not be explained by the numbers of Blacks arrested. This study assumed that police and policy makers did not target Black communities for increased "attention" and expected to find a constant rate of convictions for people arrested regardless of race. (If anything, impartial courtrooms would respond to unwarranted police intervention in Black communities with a lower rate of Black convictions and prison sentences.) But reality provided a different answer. Courtroom bias -- the decisions made by prosecutors, juries and sentencing judges -- accounted for 27.5% of the number of Blacks imprisoned in New York State.

While incarceration has devastated Black and Latino New York City residents, it has led to a tremendous boon for White rural areas. In New York State, 38 new prisons have been built since 1982, all upstate. The decline of manufacturing jobs and the difficulties faced by small farmers has led to a new rural industry: the warehousing of urban residents.

The new Five Points Supermax in Romulus is typical with 640 full-time staff and an annual operating budget of $25 million. Prisons are the main employer in many parts of upstate New York, and countless other residents work in businesses reliant on the prisons. Admittedly, land is cheaper upstate than in the city, but jobs are needed in the city as well. Readers may remember that one of the demands at the Attica prison rebellion was for the hiring of more Black and Latino guards -- something that will never happen in the rural prisons which draw their workers from the local communities.

Sources:

1. State of New York Department of Correctional Services, "The Hub System: Profile of Inmates Under Custody on January 1, 2000."
2. State of New York Department of Correctional Services, "Characteristics of New Commitments," 1999.
3. State of New York Department of Correctional Services Statistical Report for 1970.
4. "Masking the Divide: How Officially Reported Prison Statistics Distort the Racial and Ethnic Realities of Prison Growth," *National Center of Institutions and Alternatives*, May 2001.
5. "Race of Prisoners Admitted to State and Federal Institutions," *Bureau of Justice Statistics*, 1926-86.
6. Crutchfield et. al. "Analytical and Aggregation Biases in Analyses of Imprisonment: Reconciling Discrepancies in Studies of Racial Disparity," 31 *Journal of Research in Crime and Delinquency,* vol. 2, p. 178, (1994).
7. Jerome Miller, "Search and Destroy: African American Males and the Criminal Justice System," 1996.
8. Marc Mauer, *Race to Incarcerate*, 1999. Chapter 2.

VIII . 2 EXCERPTS FROM THE CONFERENCE REPORT CARD.

FOR USA: In drug cases and death penalty cases, among others, there has been clear evidence of racial bias against African-Americans, Hispanics, and other minorities. Racial profiling is an all-too common procedure in law enforcement. Minority children are also more likely to be certified as adults in the judicial system.

The judicial system strongly favors those with financial means. The poor are often not provided with competent representation. Racial bias in the selection of criminal charges by police and prosecutors, and in jury selection are all too common.

Chapter IX. Rights of Children in the Convention of the Child

§40.1 of the Convention on the Rights of the Child states that, "States Parties recognize the right of every child alleged as, accused of, or recognized as having infringed the penal law to be treated in a manner consistent with the promotion of the child's sense of dignity and worth, which reinforces the child's respect for the human rights and fundamental freedoms of others and which takes into account the child's age and the desirability of promoting the child's reintegration and the child's assuming a constructive role in society."

§40.3 of the Convention on the Rights of the Child requires:

a. The establishment of a minimum age below which children shall be presumed not to have the capacity to infringe the penal law;
b. Whenever appropriate and desirable, measures for dealing with such children without resorting to judicial proceedings, providing that human rights and legal safeguards are fully respected.

§9.3 of the Convention on the Rights of the Child states that, "States Parties shall respect the right of the child who is separated from one or both parents to maintain personal relations and direct contact with both parents on a regular basis, except if it is contrary to the child's best interests."

IX . 1 CHILD EXPLOITATION IN INDIA

Fr. Jose Pulickal, M.Th., LL.B. Dharmaram College, India

Children are the blooming buds of the garden of society. It is a significant duty on the part of each member of the society to protect these flowers from the damaging effects of excessive exposure to heat, cold, and rains, and so, too, not to pluck them to satisfy one's momentary whims. Socially, economically, and spiritually the child is the seed of the future welfare of every society, nation, and humanity at large. But the fact is that the children are being exploited by means of child labor, police harassment, and various inhuman cruelties.

The *UN Universal Declaration of Human Rights*, as we know, provided a foundation for the protection and promotion of human rights without any discrimination throughout the world. We find in the *Preamble* that the *Convention* has recognized the relevance of international co-operation for improving the living conditions of children in every nation; in particular, in the developing countries. Hence, this paper is prepared, specially keeping in mind and reflecting upon the general situation prevailing in India, a developing country, in the light of the *UN Declaration on the Rights of the Child*. The most crucial violation of rights, which the children of India encounter today, namely, child labor that, in turn, makes the child delinquent, will be the focal point of this paper.

1. Child Labor: A Brutal Violation of Rights and A Crucial Problem in India

The First Paragraph of *Article 32* of the *Convention* clearly states "the rights of the child to be protected from economic exploitation and from performing any work that is likely to be hazardous or to interfere with the child's education, or to be harmful to the child's health or physical, mental, spiritual, moral, or social development." So, also, *Article 39* obviously states the necessity of appropriate measures for the "social reintegration of a child victim of any form of neglect, exploitation, or abuse: torture or any other form of cruel, inhuman treatment ..."

India has the dubious distinction of being the nation with the largest number of child labourers in the world. It is difficult to cite a current and accurate figure for the number of child laborers in India. The ILO estimates that the number of working children between 5 and 14 years of age, in the developing countries, is 150 million, of which at least 120 million are working full time, and of these 61% are in Asia, 32% in Africa, and 7% in Latin America.[1] According to its 1981 census, the child population (6-14 years) in India was 179.9 million, of which the number of working children was 13.64 million, indicating that 7.6% of the child population were laborers.[2] According to the 1991 census the child population (5-14 years) was approximately 203.3 million, of which 11.23 million were workers, showing that 5.2% of the child population were laborers.

The fact sheet of the U.S. Agency for International Development (USAID), shockingly reveals that, in India, an estimated 44 million children are employed in hazardous and non-hazardous industries and fields endangering their physical and psychological well being.[3] Another fact is that a significant percentage of these 44 million children are bonded laborers. They are forced to work to pay off their parent's small loans (e.g., $25) from moneylenders very often for as long as six years.[4] So, also, a good number of child laborers are reported to be neither workers nor in schools (girls constitute a majority) but are engaged in activities such as collecting firewood, rag picking, and household work.[5] Neither in the school nor at work, they represent a total national waste of a sizable percentage of potential manpower at its peak formative stage, mostly ending up in juvenile delinquency on account of large-scale educational and moral deprivation.

In short, child labor ruins the childhood as well as the future life of an individual. Child labor is a pernicious practice, a denial of the joy of childhood, denial of access to social opportunities, and a concrete violation of his/her rights, which eventually impairs the personality and creativity of children. It promotes juvenile delinquencies and makes the children unhealthy, sickly, and unable to work in their adulthood. Another important side effect of child labor is that it increases adult unemployment and reduces adult wages and the result is the multiplication of poverty.[6] The UN system in its joint position views child labor as a clear violation of the child's basic right to education.[7]

---

[1] Lashmidhar, Mishra, *Child Labour in India*, Oxford University Press, 2000, p. 23.

[2] Lashmidhar, Mishra, p. 23.

[3] Cf. U.S. Agency for International Development: *Fact Sheet*.

[4] Jinesh Chandra Kulshreshtha, *Child Labour in India*, New Delhi, Ashish Pub. House.

[5] Lakshmidhar, Mishra, p. 25.

[6] Jinesh Chandra Kulshreshtha, p. 9.

[7] Lakshmidhar, Mishra, p. 239.

2. Major Causes of Child Labor

In India the major cause behind child labor is nothing but poverty. Even though children are paid much less than an adult, whatever income they receive is beneficial to the poor families. As part of and in addition to poverty, the lack of adequate and accessible sources of credit, forces poor parents to engage their children even in the harsher form of child labor, that is, bonded labour.[1] Inadequacy and accessibility of education is another important factor behind the growth of child labor in India. Child labor persists also as a result of cultural beliefs and traditions, various economic factors, and weak enforcement of existing laws that prohibit child labor.[2]

3. Government of India's Policies and Actions

As a follow up and being a party to the *UN Declaration of the Rights of the Child* (1959), India adopted the National Policy on Children in 1974. On December 2, 1992 India also ratified the *Convention on the Rights of the Child* that came into force in 1990. Important governmental measures taken towards the abolition of child labor, briefly, are the following: Central Advisory Board on Child Labor (1981), The National Child Labor Policy (1987), Child Labor Technical Advisory Committee (1986&1996), National Child Labor Projects (NCLP), Rehabilitation of Children Working in Hazardous Occupations (1994), and Assistance to Voluntary Organizations.

4. Solutions Suggested

Although the government of India has tried to implement certain measures for the elimination of child labor, their effectiveness is not very positive. Both Central and State Government Agencies, NGOs, Trade Unions, and Communication Media should be motivated towards the implementation of measures such as:

(1) Identification of child labor and enforcement of the national and international laws on the issue.
(2) Rehabilitation of child laborers and juvenile delinquents into suitable positions.
(3) Economic rehabilitation of the family with child laborers, by providing employment to adult members and improving the quality of their lives.
(4) Coordination and implementation of possible governmental projects available.
(5) Make India part of the Joint UN System (collaboration of UNICEF, UNDP, ILO, UNESC, and UNFPA), especially UN efforts for primary education.
(6) Joint venture of governments and NGOs are to be encouraged, and effective training is to be given to the NGOs.

The role of NGOs in eliminating child labor in any country is very significant, and they have to come forward voluntarily with this challenging mission.

5. Role of Prison Ministry India

Prison Ministry India, of which I am one of the delegates, is a Non Governmental Organization, coming under CBCI, fully at work in India for the reformation and

---

[1] Cf. Mitesh Badiwals. A bonded child can be released only after his/her parents make a lump sum payment that is exremely difficult for the poor people.
[2] Cf. Fact Sheet, USAID/India, *Child Labour and Human Rights.*

rehabilitation of prisoners and deviated children (juvenile delinquents). It has accomplished various effective measures for the rehabilitation of deviated children, elimination of child labor by instigating Governmental Agencies, and establishing rehabilitation programs and centers for the children in various states of India. It is by God's grace, as part of the program of PMI, that I have taken a special initiative to dedicate my own house and property for the purpose of the rehabilitation of delinquent children who are practically thrown in the fields of child exploitation. There are, at present, five centers of PMI opened for the rehabilitation of juvenile delinquents, both boys and girls, in various states of India.

PMI organizes various types of awareness programs for the public, and training programs for the volunteers by which it carries out its mission of the rehabilitation of errants. Recently, for example, PMI conducted a letter writing competition among the school children regarding the theme, Child Labor, addressing the Prime Minister of India, and letters were collected and sent to the Prime Minister, presenting the need for the abolition of child labor in India. Hence, by relying on God's power, we are proceeding with various reforms to fight against the evil powers and structures of society.

IX . 2 PRISONERS WITH LEARNING DISABILITIES

Rudy Cypser, Sc.D., Chair, CURE-New York, USA

§23.3 of the Convention on the Rights of the Child states that, "Recognizing the special needs of a disabled child, ... shall be designed to insure that the disabled child has effective access to and receives education, training, health care services, rehabilitation services, preparation for employment, and recreation opportunities in a manner conducive to the child's achieving the fullest possible social integration and individual development, including his or her cultural and spiritual development."

1. The Criminal Justice Problem.

It has been reported (by the warden of California's State Prison at Corcoran) that about one-third of prisoners are unable to perform such simple job-related tasks as locating an intersection on a street map, or identifying and entering basic information on an application. Another one-third are unable to perform slightly more difficult tasks such as writing an explanation of a billing error or entering information on an automobile maintenance form. Only about one in twenty can do things such as use a schedule to determine which bus to take.[1]

We need to ask why this is. We know that many of these people are capable of better things. Many of them are highly intelligent, or gifted in some way.

We know that youth with learning disabilities (such as dyslexia) or an emotional disturbance, or mental retardation, are arrested at higher rates than their non-disabled peers. The percentage of youth in juvenile correctional facilities who were previously in special education programs prior to their incarceration is at least three to five times the

---

[1] Letter to Mr. George M. Galarza, Warden of California State Prison-Corcoran; 30 IDELR 50 (U.S. Dept. of Education, Office of Special Education Programs, 1997).

percentage of the public school population identified as disabled.[1] Completed studies have estimated that the percentage of detained and incarcerated youth with disabilities ranges from 42 percent of all juvenile offenders in Arizona to 60 percent of all juvenile offenders in Florida and Maine.[2] Other studies of incarcerated youth reveal that as many as 70 percent suffer from disabling conditions.[3] How much of our juvenile criminal behavior has its roots in such disabilities? How much of our prison population are those who began a criminal career after failures in life and lack of self esteem due to learning disabilities? This, clearly, is a major problem. And clearly this is a resource that needs rescue. It is our duty to do so.

2. IDEA, Part of the solution.

In the USA, a start on this problem has been taken with the passage of the Individuals With Disabilities Education Act (IDEA). IDEA mandates that states provide a free and appropriate public education for all students with disabilities if the State receives Federal support for educating students with disabilities.

Once a youth has been identified as eligible for special education and related services, an Individualized Education Program (IEP) must be developed. The IEP must specifically identify the educational needs of the individual student and provide a plan for meeting those needs.

The provisions of IDEA cover all State and local juvenile and adult criminal corrections facilities. IDEA requires school districts and other public agencies to seek out all youth who may have a disability.

3. The Inadequacies.

The question is, to what extent does this law guarantee the human rights of incarcerated individuals, and to what extent is it implemented in our criminal justice system? One must conclude that the requirements of *Article 23.3* (above) are not met satisfactorily, that the legislation of IDEA is not adequate for prisoners, and that the existing laws are not adequately implemented in our juvenile detention centers, jails and prisons.

First, what disabilities are covered? Specific learning disability is defined in IDEA as a "disorder on one or more of the basic psychological processes involved in understanding or using language, spoken or written, that may manifest itself in an imperfect ability to listen, think, speak, read, write, spell, or do mathematical calculations. These well characterize our inmate population. Disabilities that are most frequently encountered among delinquents include learning disability (including various forms of dyslexia), emotional disturbance, mental retardation, other health impairment, and speech, hearing, or language impairment.

---

[1] U.S. Dept. of Education 15th Annual Report (1993).

[2] Perryman, DiGangi, and Rutherford, "Recidivism of Handicapped and Non-Handicapped Juvenile Offenders: An Exploratory Analysis (Nov. 1989).

[3] "Special Education and the Juvenile Justice System," *OJJDP Juvenile Justice Bulletin*, July 2000, NCJ 179359.

IDEA provides statutory educational guarantees only to children ages 5 to 21 with disabilities (Reauthorization of IDEA have broadened the eligibility to children from 3 to 22 years of age in most states). Moreover, there is an unfortunate exclusion from the entitlement for any youth ages 18 through 21 who, in his or her last educational placement, prior to incarceration in an adult criminal corrections facility, was not actually identified as a child with a disability and did not have an IEP. However, many offenders dropped out of school years ago and may never have had any creditable disability assessment. This exclusion can be a major weakness in the program.

The disability must be identified. There often is, however, too little effort put into the assessment of many children's disabilities and needs. Physical, mental and psychological disabilities are too often unnoticed and uncared for. Many disabilities go undetected. Youths may have a variety of impairments that are not immediately apparent. The poorest schools, from which many of our offenders come, often also do the poorest job of detecting learning deficiencies. There is too little consideration given to underlying causes, and too little commitment to counseling, special education, vocational training, or alternatives to institutional care.

When these disabilities are not properly recognized at an early age, the problems persist and may contribute to criminal behavior in later years. Many of our inmates in prisons still suffer from disabilities which society failed to recognize at earlier ages. They now pay for that neglect as well as for the crimes they committed.

It is necessary, therefore, that our adult prison population be likewise given more thorough disability evaluations and the repair of such disabilities through special education, if they are to become productive citizens.

4. Needed: A Major Shift in Correctional Education Structures

Education of prisoners is probably one of the best, if not the best tool for making productive citizens out of the students who were improperly educated or whose problems were ignored. Yet, our juvenile detention, jail and prison education systems have not been a high priority, and they constantly suffer from inadequate resources. The results have been less than needed.

Criminology experts now recognize that under current arrangements, the infrastructure needed to support quality correctional education programs are missing in many jurisdictions. Correctional education programs, with some exceptions, do not have the autonomy, administrative structure, or fiscal resources necessary to provide education for incarcerated youth, much less to meet the needs of disabled youth.[1]

It has been suggested that strengthening educational programs and ensuring that eligible youth receive special education services require that correctional education programs develop stronger ties to public school programs, gain fiscal and administrative autonomy

---

[1] "Educational Advocacy for Youth With Disabilities," in "Beyond the Walls; Improving Conditions of Confinement for Youth in Custody," OJJDP Report, http://ojjdp.ncjrs.org/PUBS/walls/sect-03.html

from the correctional agency, meet standards associated with public school programs, and fully implement the requirements of IDEA in their facilities.[5]

It has further been suggested that fiscal autonomy can be achieved through establishing a cost per pupil that is set aside in the annual budget based on the average number of students residing or detained in the facility. Education should have an independent category in the correctional budget.[6]

There can be no doubt that a revitalization of correctional education, including stronger efforts in special education for the learning disabled, can significantly reduce recidivism in our country. Lives can be saved, the costs of criminal justice and its collateral damage can be reduced, and the productivity of our nation can be improved. The resources for this must be found.

IX . 3 EXCERPTS FROM THE CONFERENCE REPORT CARDS

FOR FRANCE: In a number of prisons, where juvenile quarters are overcrowded, juveniles are detained with adults.

FOR PERU: Street children who are picked up by police often suffer degrading treatment. There are no practical alternatives to prison because of lack of infrastructure and personnel. Many times the family does not even know their child has been arrested or where he/she is. As children are sent to juvenile centers far away, some parents cannot contact them.

FOR YUGOSLAVIA: Laws are specific in prohibition, but in practice children do get exposed to torture and related acts, particularly in initial apprehensions as well as in detention. We see a very slow movement in terms of transparency. Children often get mixed with adults, and we are behind in regards to diversion systems. There is a lack of juvenile (family) specialized courts, and a lack of resources for the supervision and periodic review of custody over children.

FOR BRAZIL: Recent child legislation (Statute of Children and Adolescents) was supported strongly by social advocates, and is very progressive and forward looking. It is slowly being implemented.

FOR USA: Studies indicate that juveniles placed in adult jails and prisons are subject to more physical and sexual abuse, and the rate of juvenile suicides is much greater. While some U.S. facilities continue to isolate juveniles from adults, there is increasing pressure to adjudicate and punish children as adults. This leads to children being incarcerated in dangerous adult institutions.

Incarceration tends to destroy family relationships. If the child or parent is held in a prison, telephone contact may be non-existent or very costly. Visiting can be challenging since prisons are far from population centers, and visiting policies are often unfriendly.

---

[5] "Educational Advocacy for Youth With Disabilities," p. 6.

[6] *Ibid*, p. 6.

Chapter X.
Religion's Role in Prison in the Human Rights Documents

X . 1 RELIGIOUS RIGHTS OF MAN AND RESPONSIBILITIES OF RELIGION

Rev. Valentin Bikibili, Yaounde, Cameroon

1. Religion in the Six International Conventions

1.1. The Universal Declaration of Human Rights

Article 2 confirms that each person can have all the rights and freedoms, in particular the right and freedom of religion. *Article 18* reconsiders particularly the right to freedom of thought, conscience and religion. This right implies freedom to change religion or conviction, as well as freedom to express one's religion alone or in community.

1.2. International Pact relating to Civil and Political Rights

This pact begins, in its *Article 18*, subparagraph 1, with the *Universal Declaration of Human Rights* which guarantees the right to freedom of thought, conscience and religion and even the right to change religion.

In its *Article 20*, subparagraph 2, the *Pact* recalls that the law prohibits any call to religious hatred which constitutes a discrimination.

This *Pact* in its *Article 27* protects religious minorities which as a member of the group, should have their own culture, and the right to profess.

1.3. The International Convention on the Elimination of All the Forms of Racial Discrimination.

In its *Article 5*, the States commit to prohibit and eliminate racial discrimination in all its forms, and emphasize the rights to freedom of thought, conscience and religion.

1.4. The Convention on the Rights of the Child

This international pact proclaims that each child has all its rights and all its freedoms, including the right and the freedom of religion. In its *Article 2*, subparagraph 1, the States commit to respect the rights which are stated there apart from any consideration of religion.

Article 14 refers to (1) respect of the right of the child to freedom of thought, of conscience and of religion, (2) freedom to express its religion, and its convictions should be subjected only to restrictions which are prescribed by the law.

In *Article 29*, subparagraph d, the education of the child must prepare it to assume responsibilities for life in a spirit of comprehension, peace and tolerance, and of equality between all people and religious groups. This convention includes in its *Article 30* the protection of religious minorities.

1.5. In conclusion, the six documents forbid religious discrimination, ensure the respect of human dignity, and the right and freedom for the practice of religion, the expression of convictions, the respect of minorities, etc.

2. Prison Authorities in Cameroon

2.1. Respect of the dignity of the prisoner

Even in prison, Cameroonians continue to enjoy the human rights and fundamental freedoms stated in the *Universal Declaration*, and the precondition is that no arbitrary incarceration is authorised. Moreover, any cruel sanction, inhuman or degrading disciplinary actions are prohibited, as are punitive measures which would risk the deterioration of the physical or mental health of prisoners. Instruments of constraint such as shackles, chain etc. are never applied except in cases of absolute necessity such as a precaution against escapes, psychiatric reasons, etc.

2.2. Prisoner Reintegration

2.2.1. The purpose of preparation for social rehabilitation. The processing of condemned people must be to create in them the will and aptitude enabling them to live by respecting the law and to provide for their needs in dignity after their release. This objective of preparation to social rehabilitation has certain essential aspects:

- arrestees are separated from condemned
- the women are systematically separated from the men
- special buildings separate those condemned to death and the dangerous prisoners
- a special area is reserved for minors

However, the lack of financial means does not always allow the majority of our prisons to practice the items referred to above.

2.2.2. The preparation of professional reintegration. The required goal is to give to the prisoners training preparing them to operate their social rehabilitation. Today, in addition to an education which allows some, in particular the minors, to receive diplomas in general studies and technical training, they are prepared for professional fields such as agriculture, social education, automobile mechanics, etc.

2.3. Difficulties with which our prisons are confronted

Our prisons, built in the colonial period, weren't equipped to accommodate a very great number of prisoners. Exponential evolution of criminality and organised crime, and drug addiction have handed the penitentiary administration a great number of problems:

- overcrowded and out-dated prisons
- lack of training of the prison warders
- epidemics within the prisons
- cohabitation of the first offenders, repeat criminals and gangsters
- insufficiency of foodstuffs in the prisons
- lack of prisons in certain localities

2.4. Problems encountered by the prisoners

The prisoners in Cameroon encounter difficulties of several kinds:

- Administrative slowness in the legal procedures
- Insufficient, irregular and incomplete feeding
- Lack of work during detention
- Promiscuity due to overpopulation
- Difficulty of reintegration when leaving prison
- Bad application of the penal code due to the ignorance of the prison wardens.

Since 1982, the date of accession of President Paul Biya, the death penalty was suspended. There is no physical execution. But in the texts it still exists.

3. The Role of Religion in Prisons

3.1. Joint action of Justice and Peace and Caritas

Within the church there exists the services of Justice and Peace and Caritas. These structures are already present in the prisons with the prisoners. A joint action of these structures works for a reinforcement of defence and promotion of human rights in prison reform.

3.2. Promotion of social justice within the prisons

The penitentiary pastoral carried out by the church in prisons supplements the work started with the state within the prisons. But the church, as a promoter of social justice must reinforce what it is now doing and emphasize the following points:

- the denunciation of all the injustices which the prisoners in various countries of the world undergo
- legal assistance of the prisoners in the follow-up of their files so that the judgments are given quickly
- the respect of the rights and freedoms of the prisoners as sons of God, "Whatever the nature of your acts, you do not lose your son of God dignity"

3.3. Social services of human promotion

The prison should be regarded as a centre of humanisation of life, a medium which makes it possible for an individual to self-question and to change his life. The church should make its presence felt more in the prison by offering to the prisoners human services such as education, health, and cultural activities. These services are developing and make it possible for the prisoners to keep up hope for the future. Caritas which is in charge of human promotion should accentuate its presence in the prisons by concrete signs, testifying to the love of God the Father for the brothers in prison.

3.4. Gospel announcement

The announcement of the Gospel is the fundamental reason for the permanent presence of the church in the prisons. Freedom of worship is an inalienable basic right, for all human beings including the prisoner. By concrete acts, the church materialises the Gospel of love which, without charity is an empty love.

3.5. Actions of lobbying

The church should be "the voice of the voiceless" by trying to inform and to sensitize the authorities about the rights and freedoms of the prisoners. The church should seek to introduce its representatives into these spheres of decision-making which still do not take account of ethical values. Those values are missing in the application of certain laws.

4. Conclusion

The view of the Catholic church in Cameroon is to promote a plenary humanism. That is, the integral development of all humans and all that is human. Such humanism, associated with spiritual values and God who is the source, could apparently triumph. Admittedly humans can organise the earth without God, but without God, they may find themselves organising against humanity. Thus, we need a true humanism which is open to the absolute, in the recognition of a vocation which gives true ideas of human life.

X . 2 Prison Ministry in India

Fr. Varghese Karippery, Founder Co-ordinator, Prison Ministry India

1. Introduction

When a prisoner comes to believe in the divine, he gets power to discard old negative ways and starts to love his fellow human beings. Religion and faith in God can carry out great changes among the prisoners. In this connection, let us analyze the role of religion in prisons.[1]

2. What Is Religion?

The word 'Religion' comes from the Latin *religio*, which describes religious acts. The three verbs *relegere*, *religari*, and *re-eligere* are its possible derivations. *Relegere* means to constantly be true to, or conscientiously observe. *Relegari* means to bind oneself to one's origin and goal. *Re-eligere* means to choose again.[2] Though an acceptable definition of religion seems difficult to attain, perhaps W.H. Clerk describes it well. For him, religion is the inner experience of the individual when one senses a beyond, especially as evidenced by the effects of this experience on one's behavior when one's activity attempts to harmonize one's life with the beyond. G. Jackson states, "Religion is not a something imposed by authority from without; it is from within, a growth of the spirit, as native to the soul of man as his sense of wonder or his instinct for society."[3]

B. Lonergan states that there lies within his horizon a region for the divine, a shrine for ultimate holiness. The atheist may pronounce it empty. The agnostic may urge that he finds his investigation has been inconclusive.[4] St. Paul calls this region for the divine the indwelling God. We are the temple of the living God; man has a basic capacity for

---

[1] Varghese Karippery, "Prison Ministry India: Origin and Development," in *Prisoners: Our Own Brethren*, Varghese Karippery and Lathika [eds.], PMI Publications, Bangalore, 2000, p.14.

[2] Karl Rahner [ed.], *Sacramentum Mundi*, V, Burns and Oates, London, 1968, p.247.

[3] G. Jackson, *The Fact of Conversion*, Hodder and Stoughton, London, 1909, p.205.

[4] B. Lonergan, "Theology in Its New Context" in *A Second Collection*, Longman and Todd, London, 1974, p.233.

God. Philosophically, this consists in the question of the ultimate meaning of the dynamism of the human spirit. It may be called the immanence of grace in man.[1] Being in love with this indwelling God is the basic concern of every religion. M. Szentmartoni describes religion as a lived personal faith immersed in divine providence and according to him it is the only means to achieve integration and equilibrium of one's personality.

3. Role of Religion in Prison Reform

Inspector generals and superintendents of jail departments admit the necessity of moral instruction and the imparting of religious values. In 1994, Sri. Selvaraj, IG of prisons said, "Your service inside the prison has great influence among the prisoners. Now there is calm and peace in the jail atmosphere." In 1994 when I visited Mrs. Kiran Bedi IPS, then IG of Tihar Central Jail, Magzaze Award Winner, she said to me, "The name of the jail should be changed into Ashram. If it is Ashram, the inmates will behave like inmates of Ashram." In order to promote a positive attitude in the minds of the prisoners, she renamed the prison as Tihar Ashram. She introduced prayer methods like vipasana. In 1991 Prison Ministry India started a rehabilitation center for the released prisoners as Snahasramam with the idea that this particular center should have the style of an Ashram.

According to Ghandi, "Prisons like hospitals, are to be places of correction, reconciliation, reformation, and a center of training for rehabilitation."[2] The purpose of imprisonment is decriminalization of the criminal and the restoration of his dignity, self-esteem, and good citizenship, so that when the man emerges from the forbidding gates, he becomes a socially useful individual.[3] Security and renewal should go hand in hand; otherwise we will create more criminals in society. In the renewal process religion has to play a vital role to impart noble values to the inmates of a prison.

4. Indian Reality

The painful groaning of human beings echoes from the sufferings in the Indian prisons. The resulting challenges this puts forward can never be ignored by any citizen of the nation. Prison Ministry India (PMI) has come forward to respond to this great challenge with a new vision and mission imbibing the true Gospel spirit.[4]

In order to reach out to all the prisons in Kerala, one of the dynamics used is the formation of units attached to each prison. It consists of forty volunteers from the region. The unit functions as the nucleus emitting vital and creative energy to the prisoners and to the outside world. It works as a catalyst motivating and enriching the volunteers for the prison service.[5] Visits to the prisons are organized monthly or every fortnight or

---

[1] R.R. Viladesau, *Man's Capacity for Grace and Conversion in The Writings of Bernard Lonergan*, PUG, Roma, 1975, p.9.

[2] P.D. Mathew, "The Rights of Prisoners," *Indian Social Institute*, New Delhi, 1998, p.1.

[3] *Ibid.*, p. 5.

[4] Jose Pulickal, "New Biblical Perspectives of The Dynamic Charism of Prison Ministry in India" in *Prisoners: Our Own Brethren*, Varghese Karippery and Lathika [eds.], PMI Publications, Bangalore, 2000, p.23.

[5] Jaya F.C.C., Units "The Nucleus of Prison Ministry India" in *The Echo Souvenir* 1995, Varghese Karippery [ed.],Prison Ministry India, Bangalore, p.39.

every week according to the convenience of the members of each unit and the willingness and co-ordination of the jail authorities concerned. Sometimes we are allowed to celebrate the Eucharist in some prisons. At times we go to each cell and pray with the occupants. During the period between the prison visits, we spend our time in special prayers and fasting for the success of the visit. On the day of the visit the members gather in a particular church or prayer hall and have an intensive hour of prayer for the prisoners, and most of us come fasting. Only then, does our visit become effective. We give an hour-long program which includes prayer, songs, a skit such as an enactment of a parable from the Bible, a message, etc., which have moral value and touch their heart and conscience for a transformation. As a result once their period of punishment in the jail is over, they express their desire to go to Snehashramam (rehabilitation centers run by PMI), and they are further rehabilitated.[1]

Out of my own personal experience, I have formulated a new theory called the "Three R Theory" for the rehabilitation of prisoners. The theory says, "If a conducive atmosphere is provided, any prisoner can rise up to a normal standard of living. Every prisoner has an ardent desire to lead a better life in society, but society is not prepared to accept a prisoner, and the prisoner is not equipped to face the challenges of society. *Release, Renewal,* and *Rehabilitation* are the three main factors which play a vital role that equip a prisoner to lead a normal life."[2]

Since there are different religions in India, every caution should be taken not to disturb the emotions and religious values of each prisoner. It is sometimes disheartening to notice the attitude of negligence and indifference on the official's part concerning renewal and rehabilitation of prisoners. Society does not realize these aspects are being neglected and condemns the prisoner; but religious values can have a great role to play in the renewal and rehabilitation of prisoners.

6. Practical Suggestions

(1) Religious values have great influence in the renewal process of prisoners. Therefore, in every prison there should be moral instructors to impart good insights to the prisoners.
(2) Like the Prison Chaplaincy System, there should be pastors in every prison to get the chance to exercise religious activities inside the prison, so that prisoners may have relaxation and a new vision in their lives.
(3) In every prison there should be a special time for prayer and meditation and specialized people should be there to guide them.

Conclusion

The *UN Universal Declaration for Human Rights* leads us to believe that as prisoners are human beings, they should get the chance to lead a normal life. All offenders are

---

[1] Shalini Jose, "Unit Formation and Its Dynamics in Kerala" in *Prisoners: Our Own Brethren*, Karippery and Lathika [eds.], PMI Publications, Bangalore, 2000, p.103.
[2] Veekke, "Star of Hope in Dark Cells," *PMI Publications*, Bangalore, 2000, p.27.

members of our created human order and assisted by their input, we should plan for their release from prison and a positive relationship with society.

X . 3 THE FORMATION OF PRISONERS

Fr. Sebastian Theckanath, National Director, Prison Ministry India

Mahatma Ghandi says, "Criminals should be treated as patients in hospitals, and jails should be hospitals admitting such patients for treatment and care." Prisons are meant to reform, not punish. Jails should help in reforming prisoners. Instead, in the Indian context, we often read of custodial death of prisoners in the jail, under torture and inhumane treatment. Different types of abuses like physical harassment, humiliation, sexual abuse, alcoholism, drug abuse, etc. exist in many jails. Financial extortion from prison inmates by the officials who demand payment for receiving visitors, parole, etc., is another type of torture.

The external means may not guarantee reformation and rehabilitation. Integrated means should be adopted in a process of psychological, sociological, economical and spiritual reformation of the prisoners. Personal convictions, matured from lasting forgiveness, redemption, reconciliation and love should guide everyone involved in the process of transforming prisoners.

Ghandi, as a social reformer, analyzed the basic nature of human beings. According to him, conscious divinity is the most important feature of human nature. He subscribes to the view that there is nothing in the world that is not subject to change. In tune with this view, he regards human nature also to be dynamic and modifiable. Man can respond to the call of spirit within, can rise superior to passions, to selfishness and to violence, which belong to the brute nature and not to the immortal spirit of man. All correctional approaches start with this assumption that "*human behavior can be corrected and controlled.*"

X . 4 SOME SPIRITUAL RIGHTS OF PRISONERS

Rev. Ed Nesselhuf, Director, Prison Congregations of America, South Dakota, USA

I am a pastor of the Evangelical Lutheran Church in America. In 1984, I was called to develop a congregation in two state prisons in Maryland.This was a very novel idea at the time---our church is always going into areas where there is new population growth and developing a congregation. This is the first time we had done it in a prison.

As this developed and the members began to take responsibility for being a church within the prison, I became convinced there were some definite and distinct advantages to this model. Because a second congregation was developed and showed the same strengths and advantages, I organized Prison Congregations of America (PCA), which I now direct, as a means of promoting this congregational model in U.S. denominations and in state prisons throughout the United States.

I will list four specific "rights" which are a part of our prison congregations and which I feel are extremely reasonable and important. I speak as a member of a liturgical / sacramental Christian faith-group, but I believe these can also apply to other faith groups.

1. **The right to congregate for group worship as a faith-group**. We have learned from the 12-step groups that personal growth often happens best within a group process. The same is true of spiritual growth---it develops best within a community of faith!

2. **The right to Holy Communion (or other appropriate Sacrament), at least once a month.**

3. **The right to make contributions to charitable causes as an expression of faith.** When given an opportunity, many inmates will give generously. This is a grand opportunity for the former "takers" to become givers! Weekly offerings, CROP walks, sponsoring a child in a foreign land, and donating to special causes have been done at one time or another. This needs to be expanded! This should be a right.

4. **The right to self-expression in art work and writings, as an expression of faith.** Many inmates have developed their artistic abilities while incarcerated. Much of this art finds meaning because it is faith based. At the SDSP in Sioux Falls, SD, an auditorium has been turned into a cathedral by inmates. Six stained glass windows (5'x7') were designed and created by an inmate. New padded oak chairs were produced at a cost of $25/chair instead of $230/chair because inmates donated their time and labor in the prison shop. Artwork adorns many worship bulletins and newsletters. Crafts have been made to be sold by outside charities, the proceeds to be used by the charity. PCA annually produces a Lenten Devotional Booklet with 40 devotions, all written by inmate members of the prison congregations to be used by Christians in and out of prison. We always get rave reviews for this, for which the inmate authors are justifiably proud.

Chapter XI
Professionalism of Criminal Justice Advocates

XI . 1 CURE CHAPTER STRUCTURES

Dianne Tramutola-Lawson, Chair, Colorado CURE, Denver, Colorado

CO-CURE meets quarterly with DOC officials, including the executive director, regarding prison issues in Colorado. The meetings are open to the public for the full two hours. Also, CO-CURE is supportive of CURE being involved in advancing standards and progressive policies through membership in ACA, with a CURE representative on the Volunteer Partnerships Subcommittee and the Policy Committee of the ACA. CURE also supports more in-depth and sensitivity training for prison staff. There are many questions on how the CURE/DOC Advisory Committee meetings function in Colorado to hold prison officials accountable, and possible interest in CO-CURE and the General Assembly of an ombudsman and/or oversight committee over DOC.

XI . 2 WHY DO WE?

Kay Perry, President, CURE National, Michigan, USA

I've been asked to talk about why we do criminal justice reform work. In reflecting upon that, it seems to me that it is a two-part answer.

The first answer deals with why we got involved in the first place. Conference participants represent the typical range of reasons. Some of us are ex-prisoners. Others were drawn by the experience of having a loved one who was in prison. Some were compelled by religious beliefs, church assignments or other work-related experiences.

The second part of the answer deals with why we continue to be involved. It certainly is not the monumental progress we make. As we all know, there is simply not that much progress.

I don't know what keeps each of you involved in the work. I am only qualified to talk about why I continue this work. There are three things I look for in any job. In thinking about my work with CURE, it is those same things that keep me doing this work.

First, I want an opportunity to learn and grow. This work provides plenty of opportunity for learning and growth. I have learned a great deal since beginning this work. And I continue to learn all the time.

Second, I want to be able to make a difference. While we don't see monumental progress, I do think that we all make a difference. I believe that because of the letters we receive –some of which say, "You're the only organization that answered my letter." or simply "Thanks for being there." One of the panelists this week remembered being thanked by a prisoner – simply because he consistently smiled and greeted the prisoner in a genuinely friendly manner. It isn't just the prisoners we help; we help family members to feel less isolated and to solve problems. We do make a difference.

Third, I want to have fun. And, for me, this work is fun! It is fun because I am learning and growing. It is fun because I am making a difference. And, mostly it is fun because of the remarkable people with whom I get to work. That doesn't mean we always agree. We don't! We sometimes even argue. I would be concerned if we all agreed all the time on how to approach a problem or what our short term goals should be.

Despite the disagreements and arguments, I consider myself very fortunate to be able to work with all of you. I am grateful for your dedication, your energy, your compassion, and your being there.

Thank you! Thank you!! Thank you!!!